Walk Around

MW00632593

Fw 190A/F

By Malcolm Laing and E. Brown Ryle

Color by Don Greer

Illustrated by Ernesto Cumpian and Andrew Probert

Walk Around Number 22

squadron/signal publications

Introduction

In 1937 the Luftwaffe finalized its specifications for a new single seat fighter. Kurt Tank of Focke-Wulf submitted several proposals for this new aircraft, among which was a design using a 1550 HP, 18 cylinder, two-row, BMW 139 radial engine. This radial engine design was not considered the cutting edge of fighter development at the time, mainly due to the lower drag of the in-line engines then available for fighters. Tank persuaded the Luftwaffe the radial engine would work, pointing out in-line engines would be in heavy demand in the near future and the BMW radial engine was producing greater horsepower than the in-line engines of current Luftwaffe fighters. The Luftwaffe accepted Tank's argument and three prototypes were ordered and designated **Fw 190**.

The first Fw 190 prototypes were small, well-proportioned aircraft with wide track under-carriage, an innovative bubble canopy affording excellent pilot visibility, and a ducted spinner for engine cooling. The first aircraft had excellent handling characteristics and were liked by the pilots during flight tests; however, the testing program did not go well. The BMW 139 engine badly overheated, sending heat and fumes into the cockpit. This resulted in replacement of the fifth prototype's BMW 139 engine with a heavier, more advanced, and more powerful 1700 HP BMW 801 engine. Additionally, the aircraft received a much-redesigned fuselage and a new, larger wing. This prototype showed greatly improved performance, yet problems with engine overheating persisted.

At the time this fifth prototype underwent flight testing, the first pre-production Fw 190A-0s began service trials with II *Gruppe* (Group)/JG 26 (*Jagdgeschwader*; Fighter Wing) personnel. These work-ups did not go well, with the engine overheating being paramount, and the situation worsened to a point where the Luftwaffe recommended canceling the entire Fw 190 program! Only the testing personnel believed in the fighter's potential and after some 50 changes were made, the Fw 190A was finally accepted for service. A rough start for an aircraft which would become the backbone of the Luftwaffe's fighter force.

The first Fw 190A-1s were delivered to JG26 in June of 1941 and the introduction of the fighter into combat along the English Channel was anything except a failure. The first air-to-air conflict with the Fw 190 occurred over Dunkirk, France on 1 September 1941. The Fw 190A proved greatly superior to the Spitfire Mk V, prompting the RAF to make serious plans to steal one!

Over the next four years, the Fw 190 would progress through many upgrades and perform on all fronts in several types of missions: day and night fighter, day and night attack, long range fighter-bomber, reconnaissance, and destroyer. The aircraft was equipped to carry machine guns, cannon, bombs, rockets, cameras, and torpedoes. The *Würger* (Butcherbird) – the nickname given the Fw 190 – was capable of accomplishing all of these missions to the limits of its BMW 801 engine and the constraints of its fuel supply.

Kurt Tank had designed the aircraft from the outset to be rugged, easy to maintain, easy to build by subcontractors, and with the intention the aircraft's weight would progress upward while the design was improved. All of these factors contributed to the Fw 190's outstanding combat record and its ability to be a potent adversary against both air and ground enemies to the end of the war.

By May of 1945, Germany had produced approximately 20,000 Fw 190s from various contractors. While most of these aircraft were newly constructed, many were rebuilt from older Fw 190 airframes to later Fw 190 standards. The total number of Fw 190s built and the aircraft's wide use is a tribute to Tank's excellent engineering and the Luftwaffe's desire for the design. The Fw 190 may be considered one of the most influential and historically significant aircraft of the Second World War.

Acknowledgements

Vicki Laing	Al Ruben	Donald Caldwell
Diane Ryle	Steven Fochuk	John Houston
Lee Labar	Peter Molnar	Jennifer Houston
Ken Merrick	Charles Hugo	Ed Mautner
Alan Ranger	Jeffery Harrison	Tom Deitz
James V. Crow	Dave Wadman	Jay Thinnes

National Air and Space Museum, Washington, DC
Texas Air Museum, Rio Hondo, TX
South African National Museum of Military History, Saxonwold, South Africa

ISBN 0-89747-414-7

If you have any photographs of aircraft, armor, soldiers or ships of any nation, particularly wartime snapshots, why not share them with us and help make Squadron/Signal's books all the more interesting and complete in the future. Any photograph sent to us will be copied and the original returned. The donor will be fully credited for any photos used. Please send them to:

Squadron/Signal Publications, Inc.
1115 Crowley Drive
Carrollton, TX 75011-5010

Если у вас есть фотографии самолётов, вооружения, солдат или кораблей любой страны, особенно, снимки времён войны, поделитесь с нами и помогите сделать новые книги издательства Эскадрон/Сигнал ещё интереснее. Мы переснимем ваши фотографии и вернём оригиналы. Имена приславших снимки будут сопровождать все опубликованные фотографии. Пожалуйста, присылайте фотографии по адресу:

Squadron/Signal Publications, Inc.
1115 Crowley Drive
Carrollton, TX 75011-5010

軍用機、装甲車両、兵士、軍艦などの写真を所持しておられる方は いらっしゃいませんか？どの国のものでも結構です。作戦中に撮影されたものが特に良いのです。Squadron/Signal社の出版する刊行物において、このような写真は内容を一層充実し、興味深くすることができます。当方にお送り頂いた写真は、複写の後お返しいたします。出版物中に写真を使用した場合は、必ず提供者のお名前を明記させて頂きます。お写真は下記にご送付ください。

Squadron/Signal Publications, Inc.
1115 Crowley Drive
Carrollton, TX 75011-5010

(Front Cover) A Fw 190A-7, Brown 4, of 7 *Staffel* (Squadron), II/JG 26 leads two Fw 190A-8s in the area of Cambrai, France during early May of 1944. Brown 4 was assigned to *Oberleutnant* (1/Lt) 'Waldi' Radener and has 20 'kill' marks on the rudder.

(Previous Page) Focke-Wulf Fw 190A-8, Blue 4, *Werk Nummer* (Factory Number) 732183, is owned by John Houston and under restoration at the Texas Air Museum in Rio Hondo, Texas. This aircraft has been repainted in the markings of the Fw 190A-8 flown by Rudi Linz while assigned to 12 *Staffel*, IV/JG 5 in Norway. Linz was killed when Royal Air Force Mustangs shot him down near Herdla, Norway on 9 February 1945. The black bars on the yellow rudder indicate Linz's 70 kills. (Houston)

(Back Cover) *Ufw.* (Sgt) Friedrich Lindenlaub sits on the cockpit sill of his Fw 190A-6, White 7 (W.Nr. 550470) of I/JG 26. The fourth victory bar on the rudder was for the first B-17 Flying Fortress shot down on the Schweinfurt raid on 17 August 1943. The first three bars were for 'kills' on the Russian Front.

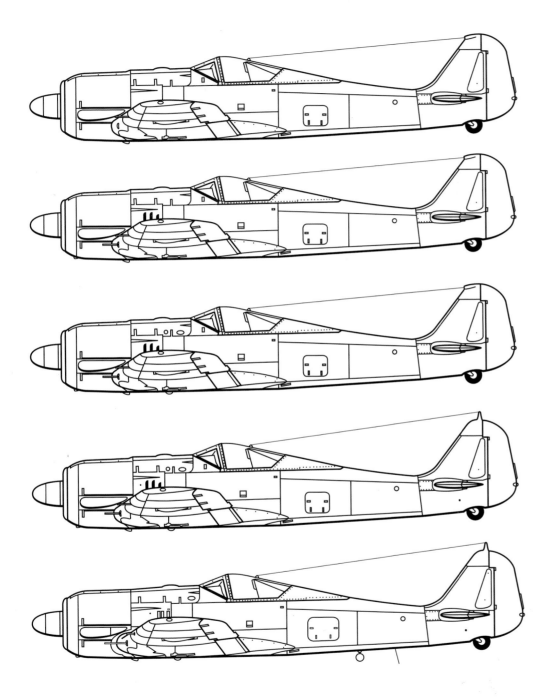

Fw 190A-1

The first production series Fw 190 entered field evaluation during the spring of 1941. After a number of modifications were made as a result of field trials, full-scale production began in the summer of 1941. The Fw 190A-1 entered service with II *Gruppe*/JG 26, where they prevailed in its first combat with opposing fighters – RAF Spitfire Mk. Vs – on 1 September 1941. The aircraft was armed with four 7.92мм MG17 machine guns and two 20мм MG FF cannon.

Fw 190A-2

The Fw 190A-2 superceded the A-1 in production in August of 1941 and joined the earlier version in service the following fall. The A-2 replaced the two wing-root-mounted 7.92мм MG17 machine guns with 20мм MG 151 cannon. The newer version was powered by a 1700 HP BMW 801D engine in place of the A-1's 1600 HP BMW 801C, with A-2s incorporating engine cooling slots immediately behind the cowling.

Fw 190A-3

The A-3 standardized on the A-2's equipment, including the BMW 801D engine and the armament, although the two wing-mounted 20мм MG FF cannon were often removed to reduce weight and increase speed. An ETC 501 rack could be mounted on the fuselage underside to carry a 79.3 gallon (300 L) drop tank or a 551.1 lb (250 KG) or 1102.3 lb (500 KG) bomb. The Fw 190A-3 entered squadron service by the spring of 1942, serving alongside the A-2s and allowing withdrawal of the A-1s from frontline use.

Fw 190A-4

The A-4 retained the A-3's basic structure; however, the newer version's FuG 16 radio resulted in the addition of a ventral antenna mast on top of the A-4's vertical stabilizer. A variety of factory and field conversion sets allowed the Fw 190A-4 to become a multi-role aircraft, capable of fighter-bomber, ground attack, photo reconnaissance, and bomber destroyer roles. The first A-4s were delivered in June of 1942 and production continued until early 1943.

Fw 190A-5

The A-5 engine and cowling were extended six inches (152.4 мм) forward to improve the aircraft's center of gravity and reduce vibration over the A-4. Adjustable fuselage engine cooling gills – introduced in late A-4s – became standard, along with solid main wheel hubs. Two ETC 500 wing racks could be installed to carry four 110.2 lb (50 KG) bombs. A number of conversion sets allowed Fw 190A-5s to undertake a variety of missions. The A-5 was superceded on the production line by the Fw 190A-6 in late 1943.

(Above) Fw 190A-6/R8, W.Nr. (*Werk Nummer*) 550214, is on display at the South African National Museum of Military History (SANMMH) in Saxonwold. This aircraft was built by the AGO plant in Obersleben in May or June of 1943. This Fw 190A-6/R8 was a night fighter equipped with a FuG (*Funk Geräte*; Radio Device) 217 *Neptun* (Neptune) J-2 radar. The fighter was coded PN+LU and was believed to have been used for testing with either the 7th or 8th *Staffel* of III/NJG 11, a night fighter unit primarily using Messerschmitt Bf 109s. This aircraft was surrendered at Leck, Germany and flown from Scheswig, Germany to Farnborough, England on 16 June 1945. The Fw 190A-6 was later displayed as a war trophy in Hyde Park, London, then stored and eventually shipped to Cape Town, South Africa aboard the SS PERTHSHIRE in October of 1946. The fighter was stored at the South African Air Force Central Flying School at Dunnottar from 1946 to 1971, then sent to No.15 Air Depot at Snake Valley and eventually transferred to the SANMMH in 1972. A restoration of this Fw 190A-6 was conducted from 1989 to 1990. The 30MM gun pods under the wings are reproductions. (Molnar & Hugo)

(Left) A replica FuG 217 *Neptun* radar antenna mount is installed on the upper starboard wing of the Fw 190A-6 experimental night fighter. Another radar mount of this design is located in the same location on the aircraft's port wing. The wing is painted RLM 74 Gray-Green (FS34086) and RLM 75 Gray-Violet (FS36122), while the black dotted lines delineate the *Nur hier betreten* (step here only) area of the wing. (Molnar & Hugo)

(Above) All paint has been removed from the Fw 190A-6 during restoration at the SAN-MMH. The ailerons and flaps have been removed for refurbishing. The aircraft's outboard cannon bay access panel, spinner, engine and cowling panels, canopy, fuselage access door, and rudder have also been removed. The landing gear legs are being painted RLM 02 Gray (FS36165). (Laing via Rubin)

(Above Right) The starboard wing leading edge was unscrewed and removed during restoration to just inboard of the main landing gear attachment point into the main spar. The leading edge attachment section for the outboard portion of the wing is a lighter weight extension of the heavy I-beam main wing spar. The main I-beam wing spar stopped just outboard of the main landing gear. (Laing via Rubin)

(Right) The gold tone of the port wheel well's rear wall indicates this part was anodized to protect the wheel wells of early Fw 190s and later Fw 190s intended for over-water or desert use. A fillet was added to the wing root leading edge from Fw 190A-5s onward when the engine type changed and the fuselage lengthened approximately 6 inches (152.5 MM). The large hole in the leading edge is for the 20MM cannon barrel and the small hole is for the collimating tube, which was used for sighting the wing cannons. The blue piping extending into the wing carried heat from the engine to warm the outboard wing cannon and ammunition, which would otherwise be frozen and unusable. (Laing via Rubin)

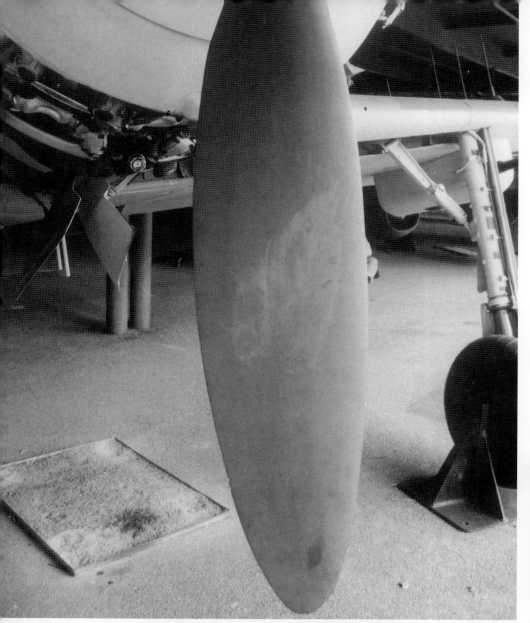

The spinner of the Fw 190A-6 was painted RLM 22 Black (FS37038) with an RLM 21 White (FS37886) spiral – correct for any Luftwaffe fighter after August of 1944. A metal data tag appears on both the spinner and the backing plate. The small oval opening in the backing plate adjusted the weights inside the base plate to balance the entire spinner. The engine cooling fan located between the spinner base plate and the engine turned at 1.72 times engine speed – three times propeller speed. (Molnar & Hugo)

The Bosch magneto mounted at the top of the engine – just behind the engine cooling fan – served as the ignition source for the BMW 801D-2 engine. The *Kommandogerat* (control unit) mounted on the port side of the engine front provided automatic control for the engine. This unit allowed the pilot to operate the Fw 190A with only one throttle lever. (Molnar & Hugo)

The Fw 190A-6's BMW 801D-2 engine turned a VDM three-bladed metal propeller, measuring 10 feet 10 inches (3.3 M) in diameter. The control unit in the engine controlled blade pitch automatically. The pilot could also manually override the control unit. The pilot could adjust the blade pitch by switching the prop control to 'manual' and using the thumb switch on the throttle to increase or decrease the prop pitch. The propeller blades were painted RLM 70 Black Green (FS34050). (Molnar & Hugo)

(Above) The exhausts for engine cylinders (from top) 14, 13, 12, and 11 are at the front of the Fw 190A-6's port exhaust area. The small hole for the engine starter crank is immediately behind the exhausts, followed by the open cooling doors. This fighter is not fitted with the fluted exhaust flame dampers or flame shields above the exhausts, which were sometimes mounted on Fw 190 night fighters. A small cooling/gun smoke opening is located at the rear of the cowling machine guns cover. (Molnar & Hugo)

(Above) The port engine cowling and wing-root 20MM gun bay doors opened for access to these areas of the Fw 190A-6. The Z-shaped part in the accessory section behind the engine is part of the engine bearer assembly, which connected the engine-mounting ring to the fuselage. The door interiors are painted RLM 02 Gray. The gun bay cover included interior bracing and mounts for seven latches. (Molnar & Hugo)

(Above) The port engine cowling door, once opened, was held in place by two restraining wires running from the top of the engine opening. The starboard cowling door is identical. Exhaust from four engine cylinders each came out the port and starboard fuselage, while the remaining six exhaust stacks were ducted under the fuselage. The engine exhaust panel was often painted black to hide the exhaust stains. (Molnar & Hugo)

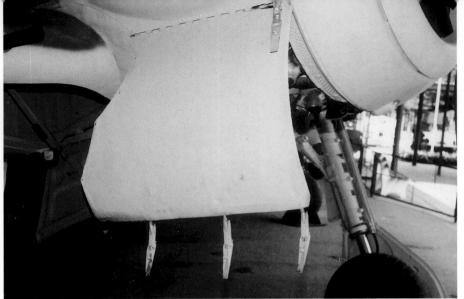

The engine and accessory areas of the Fw 190A-6 were enclosed with close-fitting doors, which opened for access by maintenance crews. The 'Z'-shaped structure in the accessory section is the bearer assembly for the BMW 801D engine. The open engine accessory access door lies just above the upper wing surface. (Molnar & Hugo)

Access to five of the BMW 801 engine's 14 cylinders was through the lower engine access door. The exhaust pipes for these cylinders were located under the engine on the aircraft's centerline. The tightly fitted engine cowling of the Fw 190A reduced drag for improved performance over rival radial-engine fighters. (Molnar & Hugo)

The underside engine access door was fastened to the cowling by three latches on the bottom and one latch at the top. The Fw 190's access doors swung on piano hinges, which allowed for minimal aerodynamic drag while enabling a wide degree of travel for the panel. The rod in this hinge was removable to allow the complete removal of the access door. (Molnar & Hugo)

The exhausts for cylinders 1, 2, 3, and 4 are mounted in front of the starboard Fw 190A-6 engine accessory section. Immediately behind the exhausts is the engine bearer assembly attachment point to the engine mounting ring. The oil filter is mounted just aft of the engine mount, and the cowl machine gun ammunition box frame is mounted on the firewall. (Molnar & Hugo)

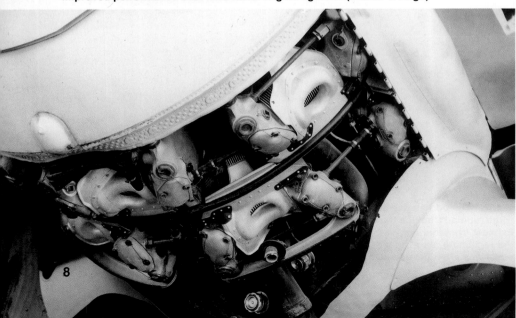

8

The BMW (*Bayernische Motoren Werke*; Bavarian Motor Works) 801D-2 engine powered the Fw 190A, F, G, and S series. The magneto is mounted on top of the gear housing on the front of the engine. The engine serial number (1151409) is stenciled on the upper side of the gear housing. (Fochuk)

BMW 801D-2 Engine

Type:	Air-cooled, 14-cylinder two-row radial
Horsepower:	1,730 HP at take-off
Displacement:	2,562 cu in (42 liters)
Bore:	6.14 in (156 MM)
Stroke:	6.14 in (156MM)
Compression ratio:	7 to 1

Fuel:	German C3 (100 octane)
Valves:	One inlet, one exhaust valve per cylinder
Valve Springs:	Three per valve
Ignition:	Dual – two Bosch ZM 14 magneto generators
Spark Plugs:	Bosch DW 240 ET 7 or Siemens 35 FU 14 two-electrode 14MM plugs, two per cylinder

Weights:	
Power Unit:	2958.6 lb (1342 KG) complete engine section
Propeller:	390.2 lb (177 KG)
Nose Bowl:	251.3 lb (114 KG) oil cooler & tank, armor, & breather valves
Cowling:	99.2 lb (45 KG) excludes nose bowl
Cooling Fan:	20.5 lb (9.3 KG)

The Fw 190A-6's canopy is fully open and the cockpit entrance ladder is extended. The radio antenna wire running from the fuselage to the main wire is slack – a normal condition when the canopy is opened. The fuselage access door is unlocked, although not open. Antennas for the FuG 16ZY DF (Direction Finder) loop (forward) and FuG 25a IFF (Identification Friend or Foe) are mounted under the fuselage. (Molnar & Hugo)

The bottom of the cockpit entrance step is designed to be flush with the fuselage when retracted for flight. This step was manually retracted by a ground crewman prior to flight. (Molnar & Hugo)

The indented rectangular panel under the port canopy sill was the hand grip used by the pilot to climb into the cockpit. A small button below and aft of the grip released the footstep under the wing-root. A kick-step covered by a spring-loaded door is located below and slightly ahead of the handgrip. (Molnar & Hugo)

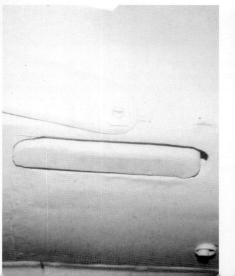

The cockpit entrance step, mounted beneath the port wing-root, was extended to allow access to the cockpit and was retracted for flight. This step was normally white with a red horizontal stripe in the middle portion. (Molnar & Hugo)

The aft fuselage and vertical tail of the Fw 190A-6 is mottled in RLM 74 Gray Green (FS34086) and RLM 75 Gray Violet (FS36122), with undersurfaces in RLM 76 Light Blue (FS36473). The FuG 25a IFF antenna is mounted under the RLM 04 Yellow (FS33637) band, while the FuG 16ZY DF loop is underneath the national insignia. (Molnar & Hugo)

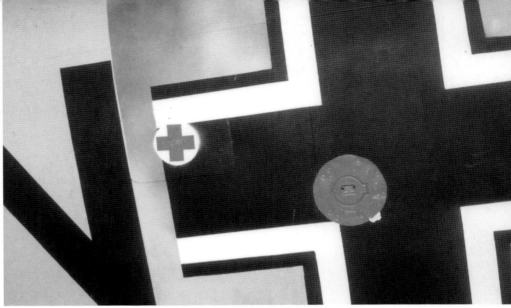

The red cross painted on a white circle indicated the location of a first aid kit behind the small starboard fuselage access door. The solid red circle inside the black cross covers the external 24V power-supply socket. (Molnar & Hugo)

Open Oxygen Filler Hatch

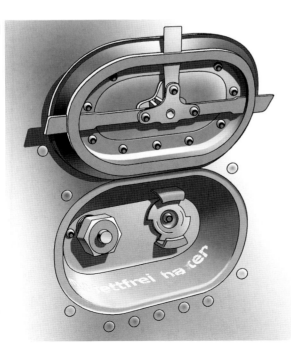

The compressed oxygen filler point hatch is located on the starboard fuselage above and behind the trailing edge of the wing. Above this hatch is a small blue panel with *Sauerstoff* (Oxygen) in white. The phrase *Ocel u. Fett frei halten* (Keep free from oil and grease) was normally seen beneath the *Sauerstoff* tag. (Molnar & Hugo)

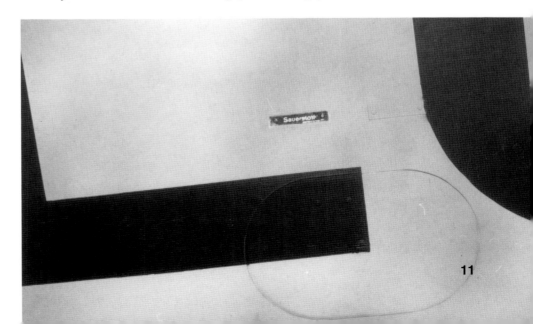

The Fw 190A-6 armored windshield's molded frame was attached with a two-one-two bolt pattern. The piping for the windshield deicing system was installed on the base and forward sides of the windshield, and were fed with fuel drawn from the cockpit 'wet line' fuel pressure gauge just prior to the fuel entering this gauge. A rectangular hand grip is placed in the starboard instrument shroud. (Molnar & Hugo)

The throttle lever is mounted in the forward section of the port cockpit console. Immediately behind the throttle are the landing gear and flap actuator controls, followed by the horizontal stabilizer trim and radio switches. The friction knob for the throttle lever is extending from the bottom of the console beneath the throttle. (Molnar & Hugo)

The Fw 190A-6 canopy crank is located on the starboard side of the cockpit, immediately aft of the instrument panel. The early 'spoon handle' canopy jettison lever is adjacent to the crank. The canopy is opened by first pulling out and turning the lever, then the crank is turned clockwise until the last tooth of the canopy drive unit is reached. A rarely seen second air vent is installed on the right side ahead of the canopy crank. (Molnar & Hugo)

The cockpit side consoles extend to the floor of the cockpit, although they do not extend forward past the instrument panel. The single throttle lever is across from the control stick grip. Almost all instruments and switches are black with red, white, and yellow piping. The A-6 port side console is little different from those on earlier model Fw 190s. (Molnar & Hugo)

This Fw 190A-6 cockpit is missing a number of parts, due to nearly 50 years of operation, storage, and display. The button on the KG 138 stick grip is for the bomb or fuel tank release. (Molnar & Hugo)

FuG 217 Radar Scope

Exact placement of other instruments was slightly altered among Fw 190A variants.

The baggage compartment aft of the pilot's seat was used to store various items according to the mission or movement of the pilot or aircraft. Radios in early Fw 190 models were mounted aft of this compartment. Later Fw 190s used this storage space to house the radios while either an 18.7 gal (70.8 L) GM-1 nitrous-oxide power boost tank or an additional 30.4 gal (115 L) fuel tank was placed aft of this compartment. (Molnar & Hugo)

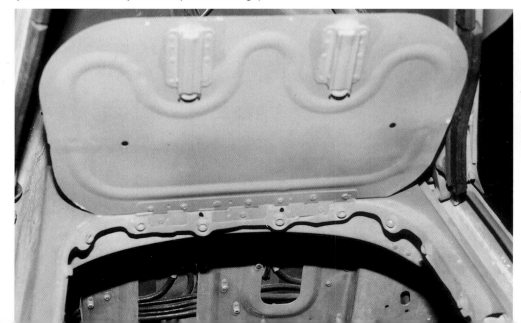

The scope for the FuG 217 radar was removed from the Fw 190A-6's upper instrument panel. Ammunition counters were located in this space on other Fw 190s. The area to the right of the radarscope normally housed the Revi 12C/D gunsight used for the Fw 190A-1 through A-6, which was still needed for night operations. The padding around the instrument panel glare shield is the original leather. American cockpit instruments were installed in place of the original German instruments during restoration. (Molnar & Hugo)

The Fw 190A-6 flaps are deployed in the 20° down position. The flaps were electrically actuated by a drive motor push rod connected to the flaps' central attachment fitting. The flaps' take-off position was 13° (+/-2°), while the landing position was 58° (+/-3°). (Molnar & Hugo)

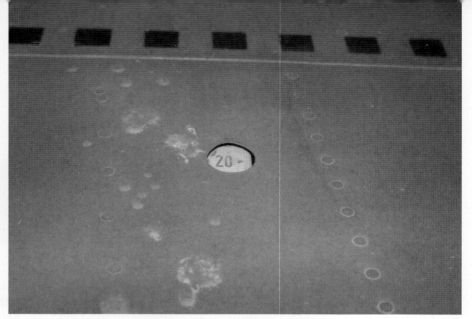

The flap mechanical position indicator – indicating 20° – is located on the upper wing above the center of the flap. This installation enabled the pilot to see the position from the cockpit. The flap mechanical position indicator was attached to the flap motor push rod. (Molnar & Hugo)

Metal
Flap
(Standard)

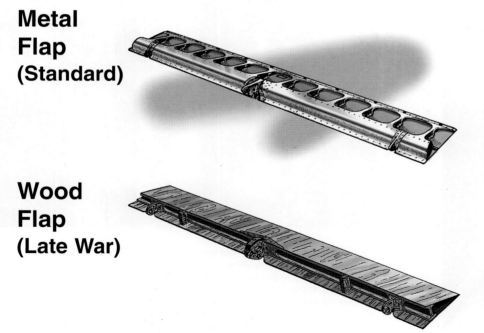

Wood
Flap
(Late War)

Flap Position Indicator

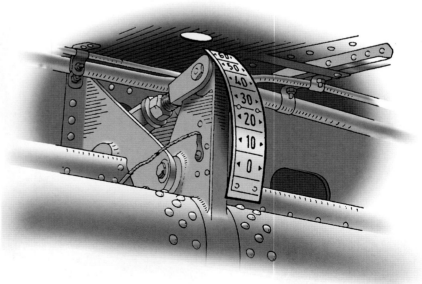

The port wing-root 20mm MG151 cannon has been removed from this Fw 190A-6; however, the mounting unit has been left in place. The forward gun support bracket is mounted on the front wall of the gun bay. The cannon's barrel passed through the hole extending through the main wing spar into the wheel well. (Molnar & Hugo)

An opening beneath the port wing-root gunbay door hinge led to the fuselage ammunition storage bin. The 250 rounds of 20mm linked ammunition passed from this bin through the opening to the weapon. Spent cannon shells were ejected through the wing bottom via the dual link-belt/cartridge case chute. The cannon's electrical firing system wiring is just aft of the EDSK-B1 distributor box. The rear wing spar composed the aft wall of the gun bay. (Molnar & Hugo)

The outboard port wing 20mm cannon opening was covered with sheet metal on this Fw 190A-6. This was a common practice late in World War II when the outboard 20mm cannons were deleted on some Fw 190s in a weight reduction measure. (Molnar & Hugo)

The red port wing tip navigation light is of a standard design for Fw 190s. The light snugly fitted into the small indentation in the one-piece wing tip with the small end of the light pointing forward. A green light was mounted on the starboard wing tip. (Molnar & Hugo)

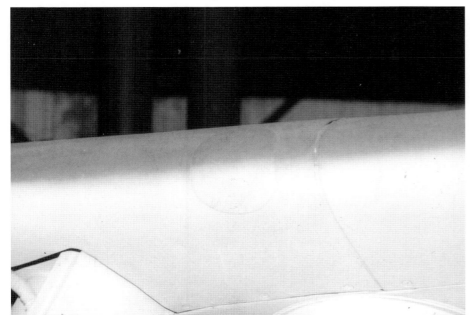

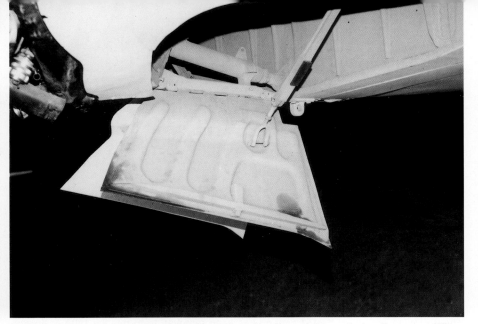

The rectangular slot aft the port main wheel well is the ejection chute for spent 20mm cartridges. The blast tube containing the cannon's barrel runs through the wheel well directly above the ejection chute. A retraction strut connects the inboard landing gear door to the wheel well. (Molnar & Hugo)

The Fw 190A-0 through A-4 used a main wheel with six circular perforations around the hub. This wheel had a snap ring and could cause injuries when the tire was changed. Late production Fw 190A-4s introduced a forged solid main wheel which was easier to produce. (Laing)

The inboard gear covers were closed by the retraction of the main landing gear. When retracted, the tire would contact the black striker plate on the wheel door upper strut. This caused the wheel door lower strut, which wrapped around the bottom of the tire, to pull the door closed. (Molnar & Hugo)

The rear side of an original Fw 190 tire/wheel assembly displays the construction used throughout the Fw 190 series. The main landing gear strut axle fit into the wheel hole. The Fw 190's main wheel tires measured 700 mm (27.6 inches) by 175 mm (6.9 inches) The wheel is painted RLM 66 Black Gray (FS36081). (Laing)

Main Landing Gear

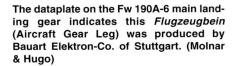

Sealed Air Jack

Rotating Drive Unit

Radius Struts

The radius strut attached to the rear of the main landing gear strut and served to raise and lower the main gear. Landing gears were typically painted RLM 02 Gray (FS36165). (Molnar & Hugo)

The dataplate on the Fw 190A-6 main landing gear indicates this *Flugzeugbein* (Aircraft Gear Leg) was produced by Bauart Elektron-Co. of Stuttgart. (Molnar & Hugo)

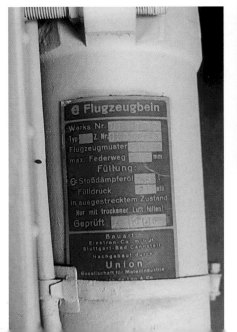

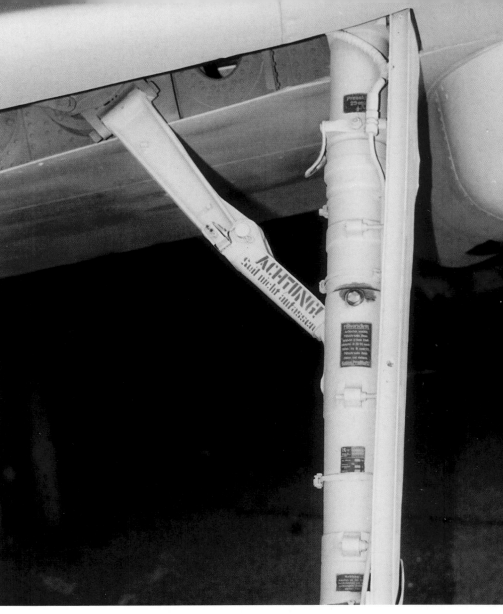

The four original metal data tags are still attached to the Fw 190A-6's port main landing gear strut. The radius strut was attached to the drive unit at the rear wall of the wheel well, and raised or lowered the landing gear when the drive unit turned. Power for the drive unit came from an electrical motor installed in the main wing spar. The stenciling on the radius strut reads *ACHTUNG! Seil nicht anfassen* (WARNING! Do not hold on cable). This warning was directed at maintenance crews tempted to push on the strut or attach a cable to it. (Molnar & Hugo)

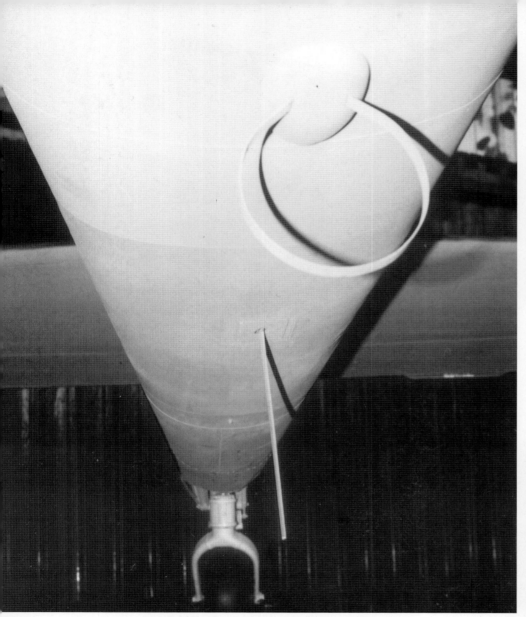

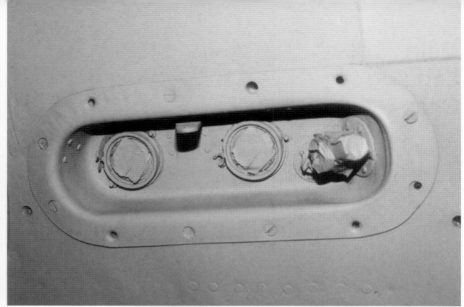

A trough located on the Fw 190A-6 fuselage underside – slightly offset to port – includes the ETC 501 stores rack electrical fittings and a fuel fitting – all are covered with tape. This trough was covered by the rear portion of the ETC 501 fairing when this rack was installed. The fuel fitting also connected with the 30.4 gal (115 L) auxiliary fuel tank located in the aft fuselage on later Fw 190s. (Molnar & Hugo)

The oval shaped lower fuselage access panel found on the Fw 190A-5/6/7 is not always depicted on drawings of such aircraft, and is smaller than the one found on the Fw190 A-8 and later aircraft. This panel has six attachment latches and can be easily removed. A U4 (*Umrüst-Bausätze*; Factory Conversion) reconnaissance camera package could be installed directly into this opening. (Molnar & Hugo)

The D/F (Direction Finding) loop antenna of the FuG (*Funk Geräte*; Radio Device) 16ZY is offset slightly to port on the Fw 190A-6's lower fuselage. The rod antenna for the FuG 25a IFF (Identification Friend or Foe), located in a square fuselage fitting, is also offset to port. The tail wheel is located aft of the IFF antenna. The aft fuselage band is RLM 04 Yellow (FS33637). (Molnar & Hugo)

Tailwheel

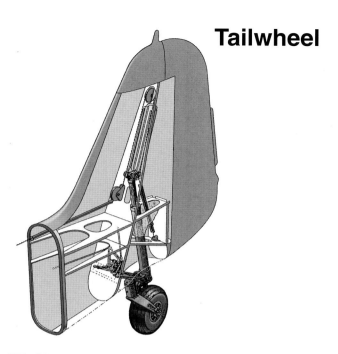

Tailwheel Retraction System

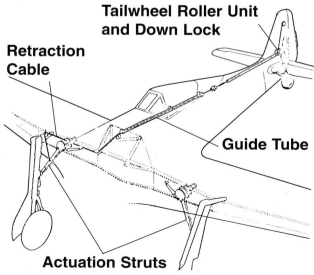

Tailwheel Roller Unit and Down Lock

Retraction Cable

Guide Tube

Actuation Struts

A complete tail wheel shock and fork assembly, about to undergo restoration, displays years of age and wear. This assembly was a later style and the air fitting was moved to the upper front portion of the shock. This tail wheel fork is turned 180° from its normal position. (Laing)

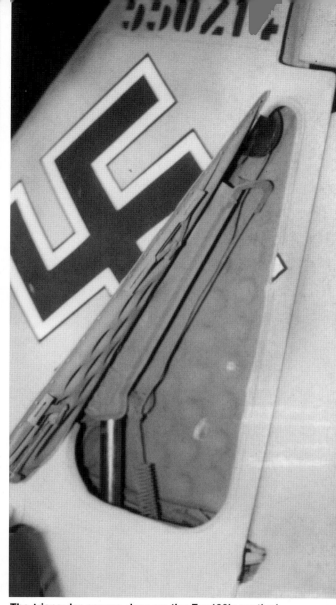

The triangular access door on the Fw 190's vertical stabilizer allowed access to the tail wheel retraction system and rudder control cables. The upper portion of the tail wheel shock absorber and the extension spring is in the lower forward portion of the housing. The tail wheel retraction wire runs over the roller at the top of the opening and proceeds to the top of the spring. (Molnar & Hugo)

(Above) Fw 190A-8, Blue 4 (W.Nr. 732183) is owned by John Houston and is currently undergoing restoration at the Texas Air Museum in Rio Hondo, Texas. This aircraft was assigned to the 12th *Staffel* of IV/JG 5 in Norway and flown by Rudi Linz, a 70-kill *Experten* (Expert). Linz was shot down and killed while engaging RAF Mustangs near Herdla, Norway on 9 February 1945. The aircraft was recovered from the crash site in sections between 1980 and 1984. (Houston)

(Below) The propeller spinner and armored cowl ring of Houston's Fw 190A-8 are painted RLM 24 Dark Blue (FS25053) with a RLM 21 White (FS37886) *Spiralschnauze* (Spiral Nose). This spiral marking was applied to the propeller spinners of German and other Axis aircraft from August of 1944 and provided a degree of head-on identification of these aircraft to Axis airmen. The Fw 190A had a wheel track of 11.5 feet (3500 MM), which made taxiing easier than with the Messerschmitt Bf 109. (Houston)

(Above) The majority of John Houston's Fw 190A-8 has been rebuilt to airworthy standards; however, the fabric coverings have not been applied to the starboard aileron and both elevators. This aircraft is also fitted with an engine section and cowling gun cover from an Fw 190A-3 undergoing restoration at the Texas Air Museum. Subsections of several Fw 190s being restored at Rio Hondo are fitted to various aircraft for work and ease of movement; thus, this is not the final configuration for this Fw 190A-8. (Houston)

(Below) Texas Air Museum volunteers move Houston's Fw 190A-8, Blue 4, across the tarmac at Rio Hondo. The aircraft is camouflaged with RLM 74 Gray-Green (FS34086) and RLM 75 Gray-Violet (FS36122) upper surfaces and RLM 76 Light Blue (FS36473) undersurfaces. The fuselage mottling is 74/75/02. The rudder is painted RLM 04 Yellow (FS33637) with the wing crosses and tail swastika in White outline form. It is intended that this Fw 190A-8 will be flown when the restoration is complete. (Houston)

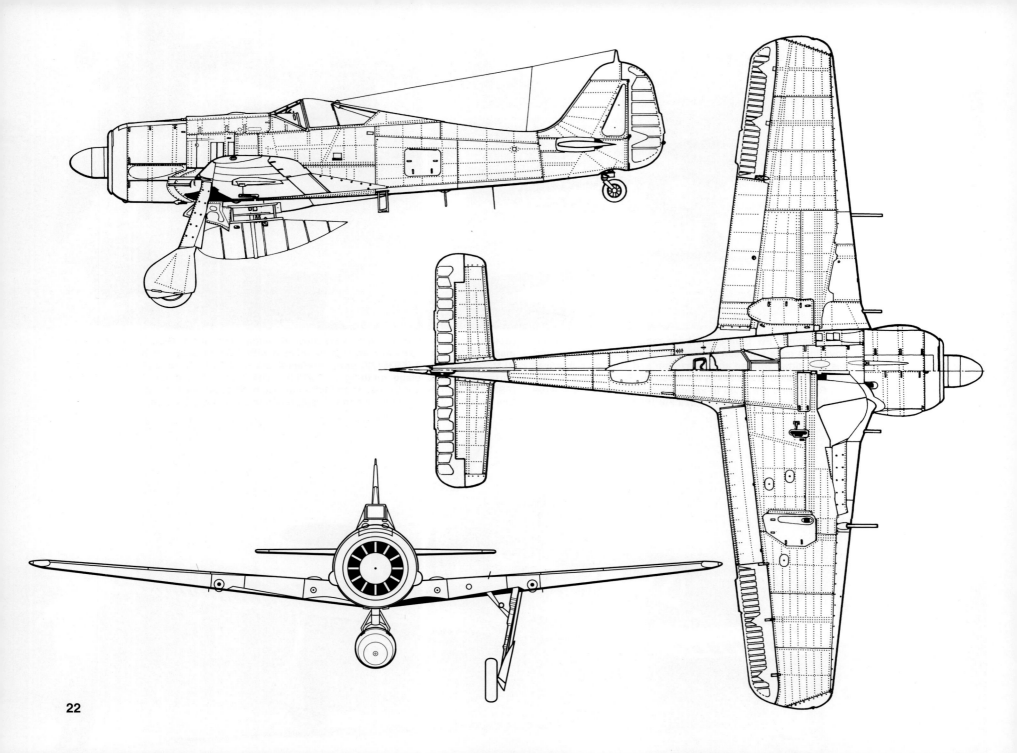

Fw 190A-6 with *Neptun* Radar

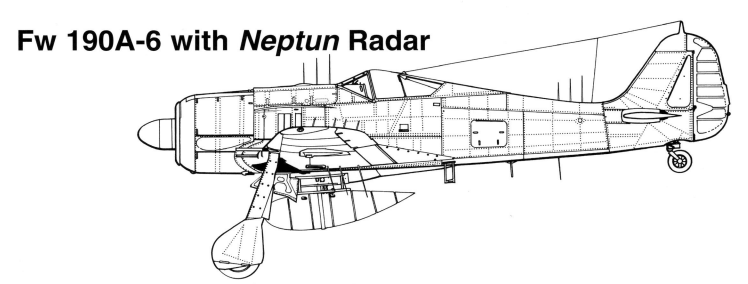

Focke-Wulf Fw 190A-6 Specifications

Wingspan: 34 feet 5 inches (10.5 M)
Length: 29 feet 4.6 inches (8.9 M)
Height: 12 feet 11 inches (3.9 M)
Empty Weight: 6393.3 pounds (2900 KG)
Maximum Weight: 9054.2 pounds (4107 KG)
Powerplant: One 1730 HP BMW 801D-2 twin-row, 14 cylinder, air-cooled radial engine

Armament: Two fuselage mounted 7.92MM MG17 machine guns with 900-1000 rounds per gun; two wing-root 20MM MG151/20E cannons with 200-250 rounds per gun; two outboard wing 20MM MG151/20E cannons with 125 rounds per gun.
Maximum Speed: 410.1 mph (660 KMH) at 22,965.9 feet (7000 M)
Service Ceiling: 34,448.8 feet (10,500 M)
Maximum Range: 310.7 miles (500 KM)

Fw 190A-8

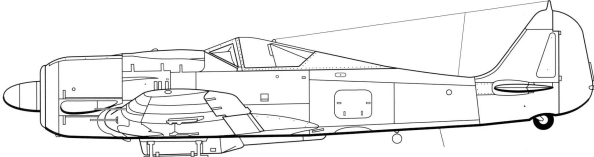

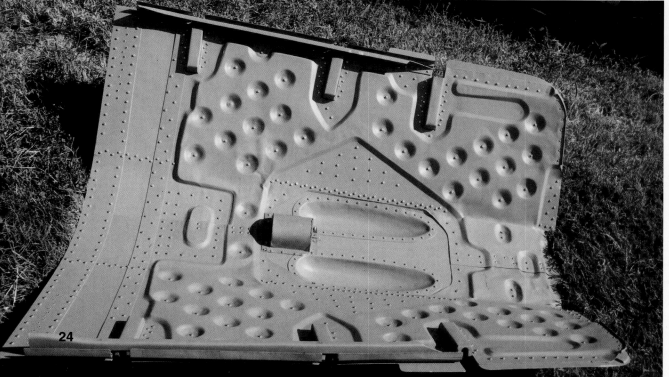

(Above) This restored Fw 190A-6 cowling machine gun cover is displayed with the forward-facing surface downward. The two blisters on top of the cover allowed clearance for the 7.92MM MG17 machine gun breech mechanisms. These blisters were enlarged when 13MM MG131 machine guns became standard equipment on the Fw 190A-7 and later versions. (Houston)

(Above Left) The cowling of Fw 190A-8/R6 (W.Nr. 733682) on display at the Imperial War Museum in Lambeth, England features aerodynamic fairings over the cowl gun openings. The cowl machine guns were removed from Fw 190s employed in some ground attack missions and for *Mistel* composite attacks using unmanned Junkers Ju 88 bombers. (Fochuk)

(Left) The interior of the Fw 190A-6 cowling machine gun cover displays the stamped 'dimple pattern' used to stiffen this panel on Fw 190A-0s through A-6s. The cylindrical object next to the two breech clearing depressions is the inside of the handhold, which was used to pull this panel open for servicing the guns. (Houston)

Fw 190 Cowl Gun System

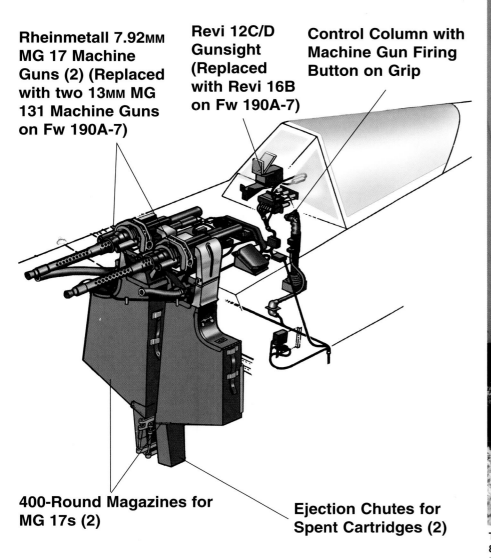

Rheinmetall 7.92MM MG 17 Machine Guns (2) (Replaced with two 13MM MG 131 Machine Guns on Fw 190A-7)

Revi 12C/D Gunsight (Replaced with Revi 16B on Fw 190A-7)

Control Column with Machine Gun Firing Button on Grip

400-Round Magazines for MG 17s (2)

Ejection Chutes for Spent Cartridges (2)

The two machine gun troughs dominate the upper engine cowling panel for the Fw 190A-8. The deepest portion of the troughs was placed at the aft end of this panel. The depth of the gun troughs and the round points at the forward portion of the troughs were standard for all Fw 190s. Openings for six latches line the sides of the panel, while a smaller latch is installed at its leading edge. (Houston)

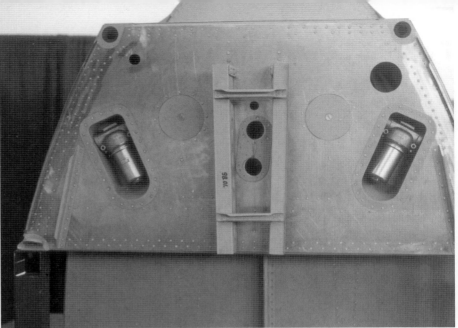

(Above) The engine bearer assembly has been removed from the firewall of the Fw 190A-8's fuselage. Two cylindrical fuel filters were installed in this bulkhead. Fuel drawn from tanks located in the lower fuselage passed through these filters before going on to the engine. The late war inside ammunition box brackets were placed in the center of the firewall. (Laing)

(Above Left) The Fw 190A's engine bearer assembly, which supported the engine mounting ring, is secured to the fuselage firewall. The hollow mounting ring was the oil reservoir for the engine control unit. Two sheet metal guide brackets for the cowling gun ammunition boxes are fitted on the outside of the firewall between the upper and lower bearing attachment points. (Laing)

(Left) The engine mounting ring and bearer assembly has been installed on an Fw 190A-3 undergoing restoration at the Texas Air Museum in Rio Hondo. The upper engine bearer attachment points were located at the outer corners of the fuselage firewall. Inside guide brackets for the cowling gun ammunition boxes are placed on the firewall's center, flanked by holes for the brake master cylinder access panels. (Laing)

(Above) The upper fuselage section of an Fw 190A-8 under restoration at Rio Hondo included space to mount two 13MM MG131 machine guns. The cowling hinged upward on two cowling attachment hinges, which allowed the panel to swing rearward and lay on the armored windshield. The hole on the starboard fuselage below the gun mounting space was the exit point for the cockpit flare gun, used for signaling when the radio was out of service or under conditions of radio silence. This hole was usually covered with cloth when the Fw 190A-8 was in operational service. (Ryle)

(Above Right) The port engine accessory panel has been installed on an Fw 190A-3 under restoration at the Texas Air Museum. The accessory panel cooling holes first appeared on the Fw 190A-2 to allow heat generated by the BMW 801 engine to escape from its tightly fitted cowling. This cooling panel was retrofitted to some Fw 190A-1s. The absence of exhaust stubs peering through the forward end of this panel indicates the engine has not been installed on this aircraft. (Ryle)

(Right) The inside of the starboard engine cowling of an Fw 190A being restored at Rio Hondo is natural metal – the original state of this surface when the part was recovered. The bulged area provided clearance for the engine air intake. A directional funnel will be placed at the bulge's aft (narrow) end when this part is fully restored for installation. (Houston)

(Above) The 'flat' canopy fitted to early Fw 190As included a piano hinge located on the top front section of the Plexiglas. This hinge allowed the plastic to flex without breaking when the canopy width varied from approximately 26 inches (66 CM) on closing to approximately 21 inches (53.3 CM) on opening. The antenna wire from the vertical stabilizer entered the canopy through the roller mounted on the top. The wire passed through the headrest brace in the aft end of the canopy and down into the fuselage, where the radio equipment was located. (Thinnes)

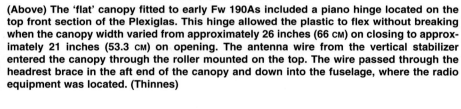

(Above Left) An Fw 190A armored windshield and canopy are test fitted on a fuselage during restoration work. The top of the windshield was the highest point of the cockpit enclosure with the standard canopy installed. The partially opened rectangular door on the side of the windshield assembly is the cockpit air vent. An armored panel with pilot's headrest is placed inside the canopy. (Laing)

(Left) The canopy's leading edge included a rubber seal to ensure a tight fit with the armored windshield. The small metal spike at the top of the leading edge fit into a hole in the rear of the windshield. This spike helped provide alignment and a rigid fit between the two assemblies. The armored headrest was attached with pivoting mounts at the bottom to the canopy's internal tube bracing. These mounts allowed the headrest to move up and down when the canopy flexed while opening or closing. (Thinnes)

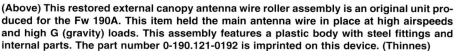

(Above) This restored external canopy antenna wire roller assembly is an original unit produced for the Fw 190A. This item held the main antenna wire in place at high airspeeds and high G (gravity) loads. This assembly features a plastic body with steel fittings and internal parts. The part number 0-190.121-0192 is imprinted on this device. (Thinnes)

(Above Right) The antenna wire roller assembly is attached to the Fw 190A's canopy by two bolts – one forward and one aft of the roller. A second piece of Plexiglas was glued onto the inner surface of the canopy where the roller assembly was placed. This added section was standard on all 'flat' Fw 190A canopies and helped provide strength and rigidity to the assembly. The antenna wire ran from the roller assembly through a slot in the metal section connected to the armored headrest into the fuselage. (Thinnes)

(Right) The antenna wire on Fw 190s fitted with 'blown hood' canopies did not enter the cockpit, unlike the antenna wire on 'flat' Fw 190 canopies. The wire attached to the canopy of this Fw 190F-8 was attached to a fitting placed on the metal divider between the two sides of the canopy. This fitting is approximately 21 inches (53.3 CM) forward from the rear of the Plexiglas canopy. The canopy is fitted to the restored Fw 190F-8 in the National Air and Space Museum's Paul E. Garber Facility in Suitland, Maryland. (Ryle)

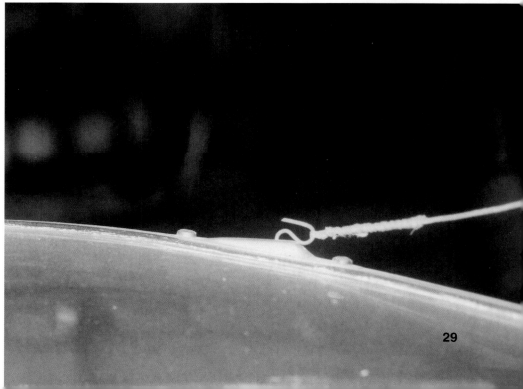

Early Flat Canopy

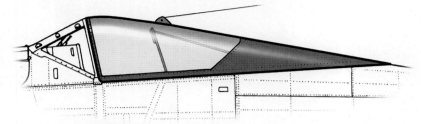

Rare Blown Canopy

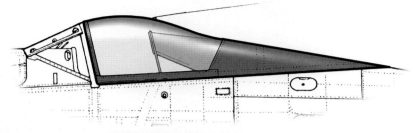

Common Flat Canopy

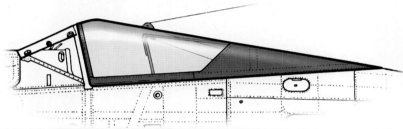

Common Blown Canopy

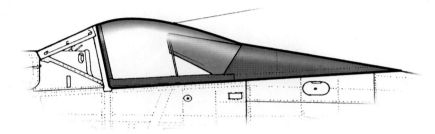

Fw 190A/F Canopy

The 'flat' canopy was used on Fw 190s from its service introduction in 1941 until the end of World War II in 1945. Several small variations of this canopy occurred during production. The 'blown hood' canopy was introduced in mid-1944 for ground attack-configured Fw 190Fs and Gs. The blown canopy featured two-piece port and starboard Plexiglas sections, which was easier to produce than the earlier 'flat' style and provided better pilot visibility. The 'blown' canopy may be seen on almost any model Fw 190 from late 1944 to the end of the war.

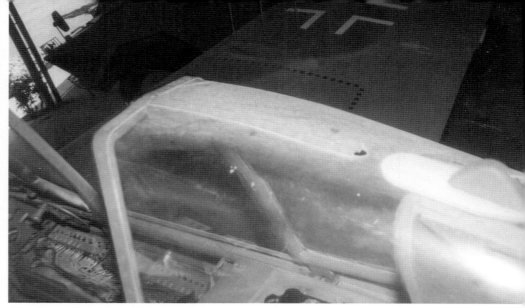

The rubber canopy seal is basically intact on this partially restored Fw 190A-6 canopy. The canopy spike protruding from the upper section of the canopy edge secures the canopy to the armored windshield. The metal exterior of the canopy front edge is connected to a piano hinge at the top to allow the Plexiglas to flex when opened or closed. (Molnar & Hugo)

The canopy opened approximately three inches (7.6 CM) past the seat's armored backplate. This position was controlled by the number of teeth on the canopy crank operated by the pilot. Screws attached the external canopy frame to the tubular internal frame. The forward roller is attached to the canopy drive section and glides inside the fuselage canopy channel. (Molnar & Hugo)

The piano hinge was mounted in a cutout on the top of the Fw 190A-6 canopy. The small hole at the rear of the hinge was a common feature of the flat Fw 190 canopy. The antenna wire roller assembly is mounted aft of the hinge and includes a Plexiglas roller support piece. (Molnar & Hugo)

The armored headrest was installed under and slightly ahead of the antenna wire roller assembly. This wire ran from the fuselage, through the canopy, to the vertical stabilizer. Each of the two small holes in the upper headrest support normally served as an anchor point for a support wire running to the aft canopy. (Molnar & Hugo)

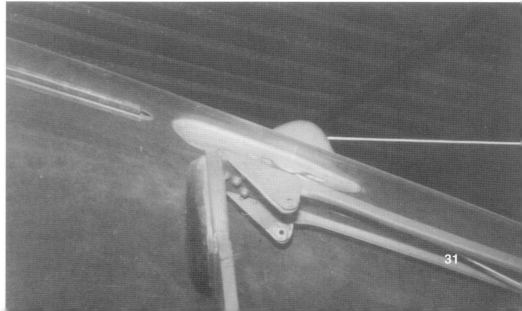

This Fw 190F-8 armored headrest was made in three sections: A bottom armored plate, a stamped sheet metal cover at the top, and a front cover with headrest. Two simple late war pivot mounts attached the lower armored plate to the canopy bottom. The English translation of the placard reads: Attention! Release of the canopy by explosive charge. Do not touch release lever. In case of a test first secure the striker. (Ryle)

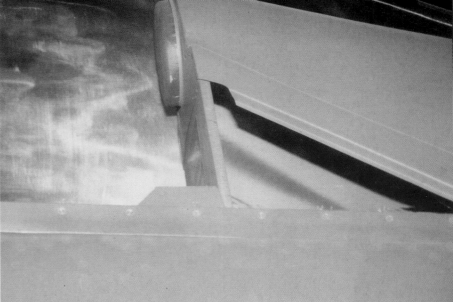

The headrest on Fw 190s equipped with 'blown hood' canopies featured a non-moving upper support, unlike the moving headrest support used with the earlier 'flat' canopies. The upper support and the front cover were made from stamped sheet metal, with the front cover attached with spot welds. (Ryle)

The armored headrest stops just aft of the canopy channels when the canopy is fully open. These channels have upsloping ends, which allow the canopy rollers to free themselves when an explosive charge jettisons the canopy. (Ryle)

Fw 190s equipped with 'blown hood' canopies featured a non-moving upper headrest support, which connected the headrest to the canopy rear. Double rows of screws secured the Plexiglas sections to the canopy frame. (Ryle)

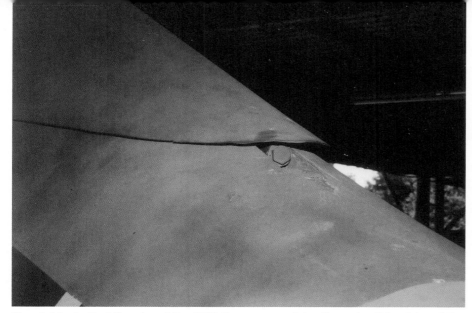

The slot just aft of the closed Fw 190A-6 canopy contains the outer firing tube of the canopy emergency jettison system, which employed an explosive charge to blow the canopy off the fuselage. This slot is centered on the fuselage spine, while the spine panel seam is offset to starboard – a configuration found on all Fw 190s. (Molnar & Hugo)

The outer firing tube and its attachment point protrude from the opened Fw 190A-6 canopy. This tube fitted over the inner firing tube, which contained a 26MM flare gun blank for an explosive charge. The charge was located behind the pilot's seat and activated by pressing the jettison lever on the canopy drive unit in the cockpit. This lever released a firing pin and the channeled explosion propelled the canopy rearward off the aircraft. (Molnar & Hugo)

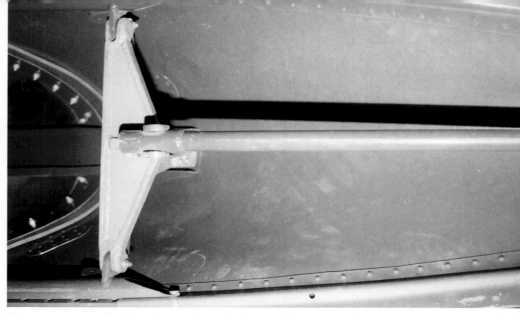

The outer canopy ejection tube ran along the bottom of the Fw 190 'flat' canopy and was attached to the cross bracing located at the aft end of the canopy's tubular frame. This cross bracing was the attachment point for the upper support and lateral wire supports of the armored headrest. The aft end of the tubular frame is attached to the formed metal internal canopy bracing. (Laing)

The aft cross bracing of the open Fw 190A-6 canopy flexes minutely when the canopy is in this position. This slight flexing means the canopy section maintains its width in the open position, while the canopy flexes approximately five inches (12.7 CM) in width at its forward edge and less at the armored headrest. (Molnar & Hugo)

33

The Fw 190A pilot's seat's four rollers fit into seat guide channels located at the aft sides of the cockpit. Two small levers placed on the top rollers adjusted the seat up and down. Pushing the levers in or out allowed locking studs to retract or extend into one of six holes placed inside the seat guide channels. (Laing)

Two shoulder harness fittings were mounted on the aft upper cockpit armor just forward and below the armored headrest. These fittings secured the pilot's shoulder straps, which connected with the port and starboard seat belts. The shoulder belt fittings used on this Fw 190A undergoing restoration are original. (Laing)

The Fw 190A pilot's seat consisted of a Dural (aluminum alloy) pan riveted to an armored back plate with two attachment/adjustment rollers per side. The seat adjustment levers (not visible) protrude upward from the upper pair of rollers. All four rollers fit into the two seat guide channels fitted into the sides of the aft cockpit area. (Laing)

Pilot's Seat

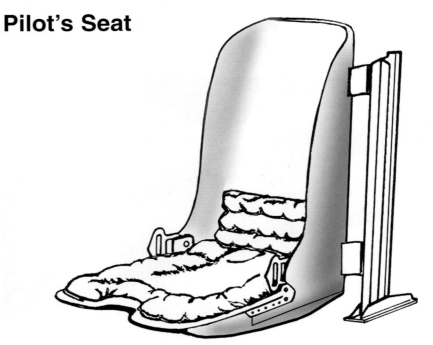

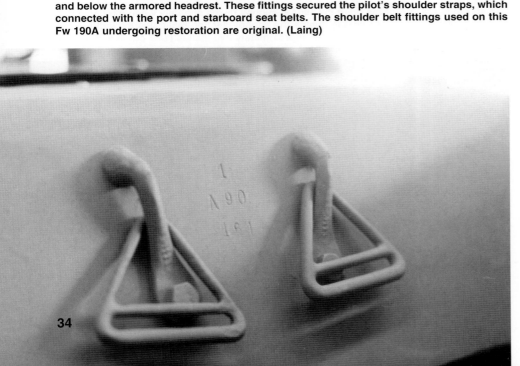

Fw 190A-7/8/9 Fuselage

Early Fw 190A Fuselage Door

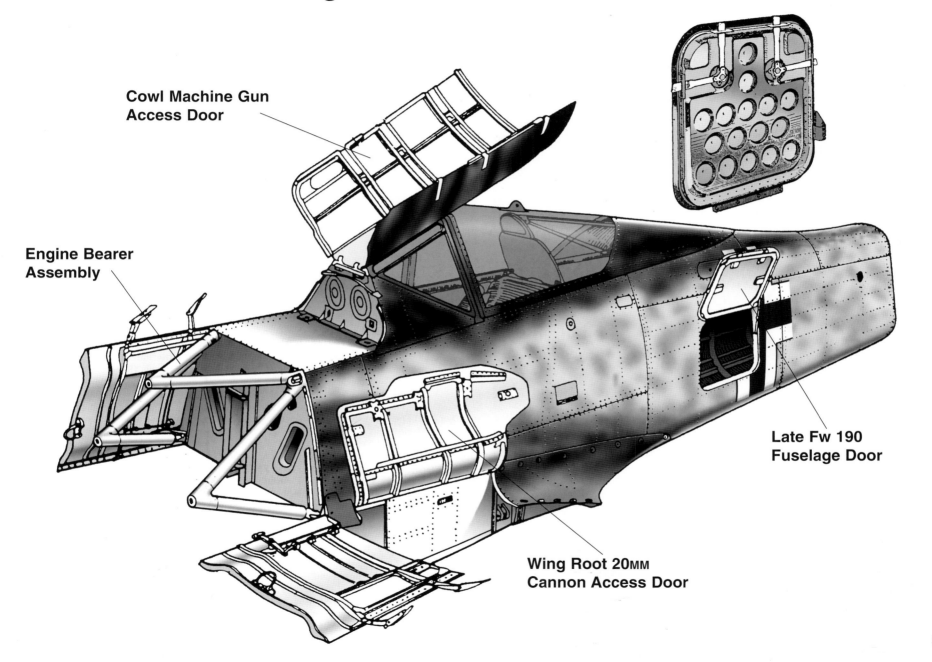

Cowl Machine Gun Access Door

Engine Bearer Assembly

Late Fw 190 Fuselage Door

Wing Root 20MM Cannon Access Door

(Above) An outboard section of an Fw 190A-3 starboard wing recovered in Norway reveals wear from nearly 50 years in a derelict state. The wing received a factory-applied coat of RLM 76 Light Blue followed by a single application of RLM 75 Gray-Violet in the standard camouflage pattern for the Fw 190A. The black and white wing cross was applied over the camouflage. This aircraft belonged to JG5 and came from the final batch of Fw 190A-3s built. The wing has since been restored by the Texas Air Museum. (Ryle)

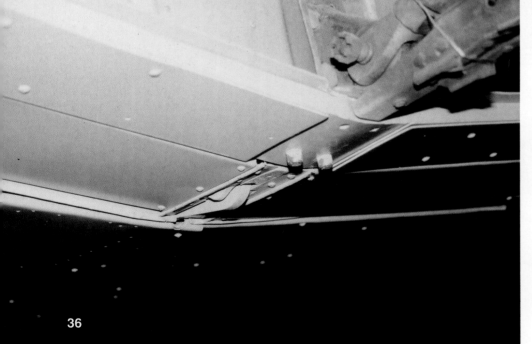

(Above Left) The port elevator has been installed on an Fw 190A-3 under restoration at the Texas Air Museum in Rio Hondo; however, the elevator trim tab has not yet been painted red. The elevators – like the rudder and ailerons – consisted of metal frames covered with doped fabric, which was then painted the camouflage colors. The aircraft was painted RLM 74 Gray-Green (FS34086) and RLM 75 Gray-Violet (FS36122) on the upper surfaces with RLM 76 Light Blue (FS36473) undersurfaces. This Fw 190F-8, White 1, displays a white disc aft of the national insignia, which indicated assignment to the 9 *Staffel* (Squadron), IV *Gruppe* (Group) of a *Jagdgeschwader* (Fighter Wing). (Laing)

(Left) The small aerodynamic bump on the centerline of an Fw 190A-3 – just behind the wheel well – was common to all Fw 190s. Just ahead of this bump is the forward attachment/pivot point of the fuel tank cover panel over the fuselage fuel tank bay. This fitting is directly between the two access panels for the wing-root 20MM cannon ammunition boxes. The pivot point was covered when an ETC (*Einzelträger C-munition*; Single Rack with High-Explosive Bomb) 501 bomb rack was installed on the aircraft. (Ryle)

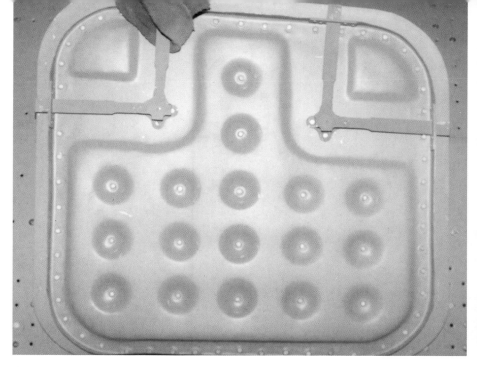

(Above) This fuselage access door on an Fw 190A-3 under restoration at Rio Hondo, Texas was the type of door used on Fw 190A-0s through A-4s. This hatch was rectangular and set low into the port fuselage aft of the cockpit. The interior 'waffle pattern' stiffening was common to early Fw 190s. The door swung upward on the hinge and four latching points secured the door to the fuselage. (Houston)

(Above Right) Restoration work at the Texas Air Museum is bringing this Fw 190A-3 tail assembly to airworthy standards. A series of canted ribs in the forward section of the vertical stabilizer provides strength and rigidity to the structure. The framework is covered with a bolted on leading edge and aluminum riveted side skinning – the starboard side skin has been installed on this example. The starboard triangular stamped section has been fitted. The electric motor for adjusting the horizontal stabilizer incidence will be installed at the base of the vertical stabilizer. (Laing)

(Right) A partially assembled port horizontal stabilizer and elevator assembly is test fitted on an Fw 190A-8 at Rio Hondo. The metal parts have been given a primer coat of zinc chromate. The elevator's fabric covering will be sewed with wire onto the metal framework, then tape will be applied to the edges. The fabric is shrunk with dope prior to painting the elevator in the Fw 190's camouflage colors. (Laing)

Fw 190A-7/8 Armament System

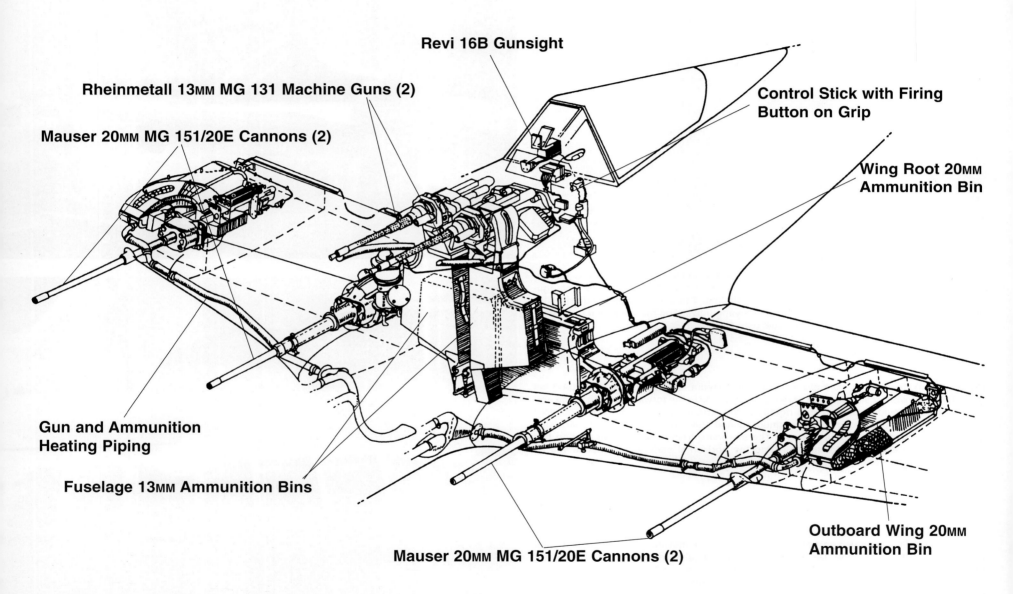

Revi 16B Gunsight

Rheinmetall 13MM MG 131 Machine Guns (2)

Mauser 20MM MG 151/20E Cannons (2)

Control Stick with Firing Button on Grip

Wing Root 20MM Ammunition Bin

Gun and Ammunition Heating Piping

Fuselage 13MM Ammunition Bins

Mauser 20MM MG 151/20E Cannons (2)

Outboard Wing 20MM Ammunition Bin

Fw 190F-1 through F-3

Fw 190F-1

The Fw 190F series was developed for the close support role, replacing the obsolete Junkers Ju 87 Stuka dive bomber. The Fw 190F-1 was derived from the Fw 190A-4/U4 *Jabo* (*Jagdbomber*; Fighter-Bomber) conversion, in which the outboard wing 20MM cannons were deleted. Gun armament on this and subsequent Fw 190Fs was reduced to a pair of fuselage mounted 7.92MM MG 17 machine guns and two wing-root mounted 20MM MG 151 cannons. An ETC 501 ventral bomb rack was installed to carry a single 551.1 lb (250 KG) or 1102.3 lb (500 KG) bomb, or four 110.2 lb (50 KG) bombs. Internal armor was added to the engine cowling, fuselage fuel tanks, and cockpit for protection against enemy fire. Approximately 30 Fw 190F-1s were built through the middle of 1943, and the majority of these served on the Eastern Front.

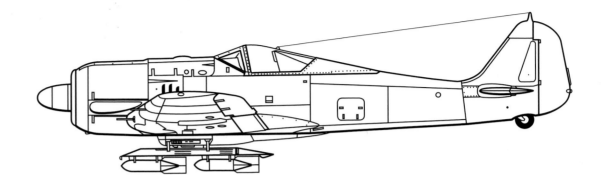

Fw 190F-2

The Fw 190F-2 was a derivative of the Fw 190A-5/U3 factory conversion model, which retained the A-5's six inch (152.5 MM) long fuselage extension over the Fw 190A-4. Internal and external armament remained the same as for the Fw 190F-1, and the internal armor protection was also retained. Many F-2s were built with side cowling air intakes equipped with tropical filters to keep sand and dust out of the engine. Total Fw 190F-2 production came to 270 airframes. Although most of these aircraft were assigned to the Eastern Front, several were deployed to the Mediterranean theater.

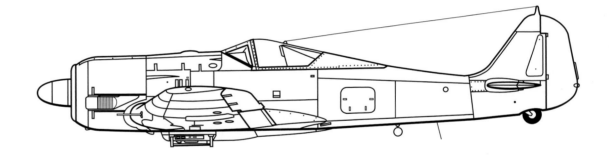

Fw 190F-3

The Fw 190A-5/U17 factory conversion became the basis of the Fw 190F-3 ground attack aircraft. This aircraft added four ETC 50 bomb racks under the outboard wings – two racks per wing – to each carry a 50 KG bomb. The remaining armament and armor protection was retained from the Fw 190F-2. Tropical cowling filters were fitted to many F-3s and provision was made for installing a gun camera in the port wing leading edge. Arado built 270 Fw 190F-3s, the majority of which saw service on the Eastern Front. Production of the Fw 190F-4, F-5, and F-7 was cancelled in favor of the Fw 190G long-range fighter-bomber; however, Fw 190F series production resumed with the Fw 190F-8 in 1944.

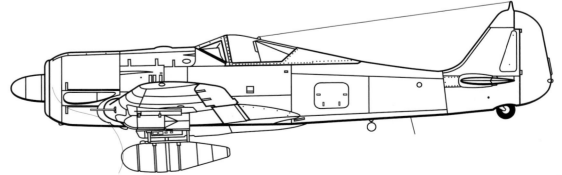

(Above) The National Air and Space Museum's Fw 190F-8 was painted RLM 70 Black Green (FS34050) and RLM 75 Gray Violet (FS36122) on the upper surfaces, with under surfaces finished in RLM 76 Light Gray (FS36473). During restoration, it was found this aircraft had tan upper surfaces over light gray under surfaces, indicating the possible use of this aircraft in the Balkans or the Mediterranean. This paint may have been applied to the airframe when this was an Fw 190A-4; however, this is not known for sure. The port side fuselage panel was upgraded to A-5 through A-9 style during rebuilding to F-8 standard with a larger fuselage access door. (Ryle)

(Above Left) Fw 190F-8/R1, White 7 (W.Nr. 931884) was built as an A-4 (W.Nr. 640069) by Arado at Warnemunde, Germany. In early 1944 this aircraft was rebuilt to F-8 standards by Fieseler and its *Werk Nummer* (Factory Number) changed to 931884. This Fw 190F-8 saw action with I/SG 2 (*Schlachtgeschwader*; Attack Wing) on the Eastern Front against the Soviets in 1944 and 1945. The aircraft was captured by US forces in 1945 and assigned the Foreign Aircraft Evaluation code FE-117. After the Fw 190F-8 arrived in the US, the Smithsonian Institution's National Air and Space Museum (NASM) acquired the aircraft and placed it in storage until the airframe was restored between 1980 and 1983. This Fw 190F-8 is displayed at NASM's Paul E. Garber Facility in Suitland, Maryland, just outside Washington, DC. (Ryle)

(Left) The last three digits of the Fw 190F-8's *Werk Nummer* – 884 – were hand-painted in black on the tail. The data tag inside the fuselage retains the original Fw 190F-4 W.Nr. of 640069. NASM restorers discovered this aircraft was coded White 7 and Yellow 10 in different camouflage schemes during World War II. The RLM 04 Yellow (FS33637) aft fuselage band indicated assignment to the Eastern Front. (Ryle)

(Above) The Fw 190F-8 retained the same engine cowling and propeller spinner as the Fw 190As and earlier Fs. The spinner of the NASM's aircraft is painted RLM 22 Black (FS37038) with an RLM 21 White (FS37886) spiral for head-on recognition of Axis aircraft. The propeller blades are RLM 70 Black Green (FS34050). The forward cowling ring is protected by 6.5MM of armor, while the cowl has 5.5MM armor. The 1730 HP BMW 801D-2 14-cylinder air-cooled radial engine and its associated plumbing are mounted behind the 12-blade cooling fan retained from earlier radial-engined Fw 190s. One 20MM MG 151 cannon is mounted in each wing root. (Ryle)

(Right) Fw 190Fs were fitted with three-bladed wooden propellers, whose paddle blades were designed to move large volumes of air. The blade is made from 1/32nd inch (0.85 CM) sheets of laminated wood glued together. The black painted brass leading edge was carefully inlayed into the wood. The wooden blade was covered with cloth, which was glued or doped to the wood, painted RLM 70 Black Green, and covered with a clear waterproof finish. The steel cuff at the base of the propeller blade fitted into the propeller hub. The Fw 190's propeller measured 10 feet 10 inches (3.3 M) in diameter, with automatic pitch control performed by the BMW 801 engine's control unit. Manual pitch control through electrical power was possible by the pilot's switching to manual control and using the thumb switch on the throttle to increase or decrease propeller pitch. (Ryle)

41

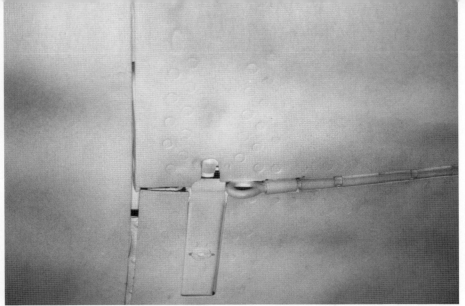

The two lower engine cowling doors are closed on this Fw 190F-8 and the three latches are secured in place. An oil drain valve is covered by a small bump just ahead of the cowling door. The engine oil sump drain is fitted to the port door, with an access port further aft on this hatch. The lower exhaust bank and number 8 cylinder exhaust port cutout are placed at the aft edge of the engine cowling. (Mautner)

The lower engine exhaust bank for the (from right) 6, 5, 7, and 10/9 cylinders is on the Fw 190F-8's centerline. The 6 and 5 cylinder ports are vertical, the 7 and 10/9 stacks are horizontal, and the combined 10/9 port is the largest. The hot exhaust gases were channeled along the fuselage centerline by the shape of the exhaust area and the fixed fairing on the inside of the wheel wells. (Mautner)

The lower engine cowling swings from the side cowling by a piano hinge. The form-fitting forward latch – one of three on this door – keeps the panel closed in flight and helps keep the hinge rod in place between these two panels. By pulling the rod forward using its small circular end, the entire lower cowling panel could be removed. (Ryle)

Fw 190A/F Exhaust Arrangement

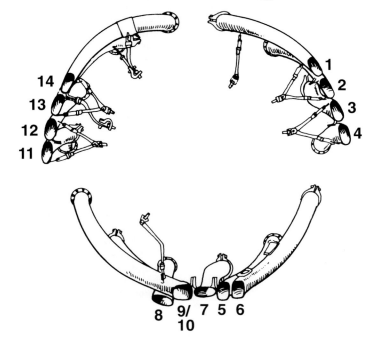

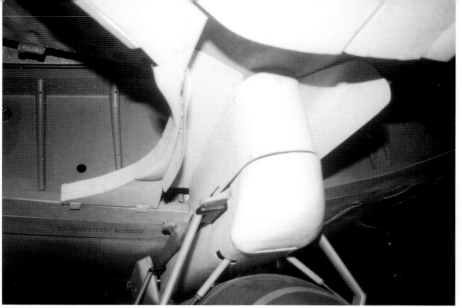

This ETC (*Einzelträger C-munition*; Single Rack with High-Explosive Bomb) 501 bomb rack and fairing was found in Norway and was originally installed on one of the Fw 190s now at the Texas Air Museum. It is currently installed on the NASM's Fw 190F-8. Small-fixed fairings left and right of the rack were designed to channel gases from the lower exhaust bank away from the landing gear tires. The inner landing gear doors could not be used when the ETC 501 was installed. (Ryle)

When the ETC 501 bomb rack was installed on the Fw 190A-8/F-8, the rack was moved forward eight inches (20.3 CM) from the location on previous Fw 190s. The move was required to rebalance the aircraft due to the new 30.4 gallon (115 L) auxiliary fuel tank in the fuselage aft of the pilot's seat. The 250 SC bomb is painted RLM 66 Black Gray (FS36081) with red stripes. Other standard colors for German bombs were RLM 02 Gray and RLM 76 Light Blue. (Ryle)

An ETC 501 rack and carrier unit is installed on the Fw 190A-8 displayed at the Imperial War Museum in Lambeth, England. The three-piece aerodynamic fairing usually fitted to the rack is not installed here. The rack is set up for a 79.3 gallon (300 L) drop tank; however, none of the necessary wiring or plumbing is installed. (Fochuk)

ETC 501 with Drop Tank

ETC 501 with Bomb

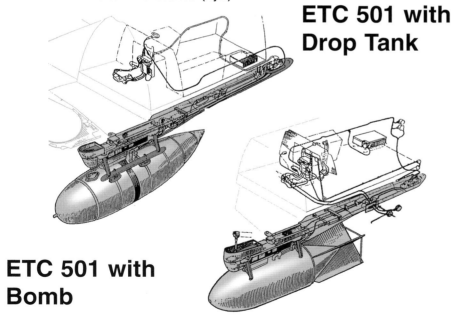

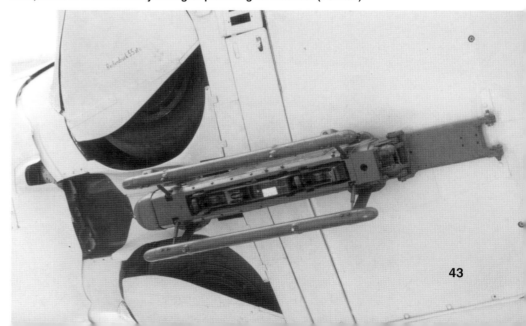

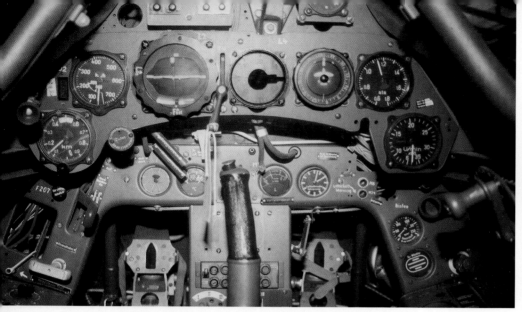

The lower section of the Fw 190F-8's instrument panel houses auxiliary instruments. These instruments are (L-R): Engine starter brushes withdrawal button; fuel tank selector switch; fuel and oil pressure; oil temperature; fuel gauge; propeller pitch; fuel low level light; rear (fuel) tank switch-over light; fuel gauge selector switch; flare gun port; oxygen pressure gauge; oxygen flow gauge; and oxygen flow valve. (Ryle)

Alongside the pilot's seat in the Fw 190F-8 cockpit is the port console. Console components are (from Aft): Primer fuel pump handle; FuG 16ZY radio volume control; radio tuner; frequency selector; horizontal stabilizer trim switch; landing gear and flap actuator buttons; throttle lever with thumb actuated propeller pitch control; horizontal stabilizer trim indicator; magneto switch; and instrument panel lighting dimmer control. (Ryle)

This Fw 190 main instrument panel is painted RLM 66 Black Gray and the instruments are black with white markings. These instruments are (from Left): Pressure altimeter; pitot tube heater light; airspeed indicator; artificial horizon; vertical speed indicator; repeater compass; manifold pressure indicator; and tachometer. (Ryle)

The rudder pedals hang from behind the instrument panel and have push rods attached to their outside edge. These rods proceed down the fuselage sides to the rudder differential unit, then to the rudder. The pedals have the main landing gear brake system attached to the rear sides, which is activated by toe pressure on the top of the pedals. The rudder control lock strap is attached to the left rudder pedal arm. The Fw 190F-8 armament panel is forward of the control stick. (Ryle)

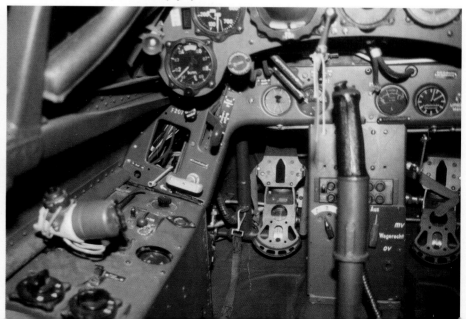

The bottom of the Revi 16B gun sight and mount is placed under the instrument glare shield. The vertical indicators to the left of the gun sight are the round counters for the cannon and machine guns, indicating to the pilot how much ammunition per gun he has remaining. The instrument to the right of the Revi mount is the FuG 16ZY homing indicator. (Ryle)

The map case and its leather strap are alongside the starboard console of the Fw 190F-8 cockpit. This position allowed ease of pilot access to maps during a flight. The control stick has a rubber boot (dust cover) over its base. German fighter aircraft cockpits were normally painted RLM 66 Black Gray (FS36081). (Ryle)

The Fw 190F-8's canopy drive crank and jettison lever are mounted above the starboard console. The silver rod along the fuselage side is the mechanical attachment to the firing pin of the explosive charge used to jettison the canopy. Console items are (from Aft): Circuit breakers; starter switch; and mount for the cockpit clock, which is missing here. (Ryle)

The Fw 190F-8 pilot's seat and lap belts remained generally the same throughout the Fw 190's service. Each lap belt was equipped with a thick, triangular chafing pad. The aluminum seat pan – the lower portion of the seat – was riveted to the 8MM armored seat back plate. This pan usually had a seat cushion installed. The upper rear portion of the pan has a shelf for the pilot's parachute to rest on. (Ryle)

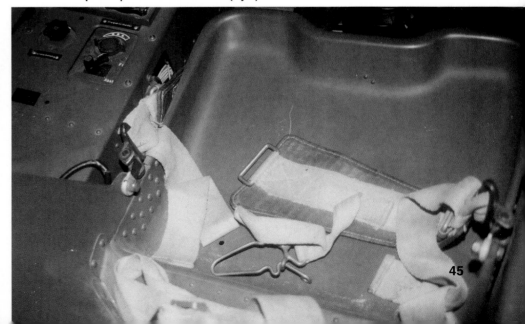

45

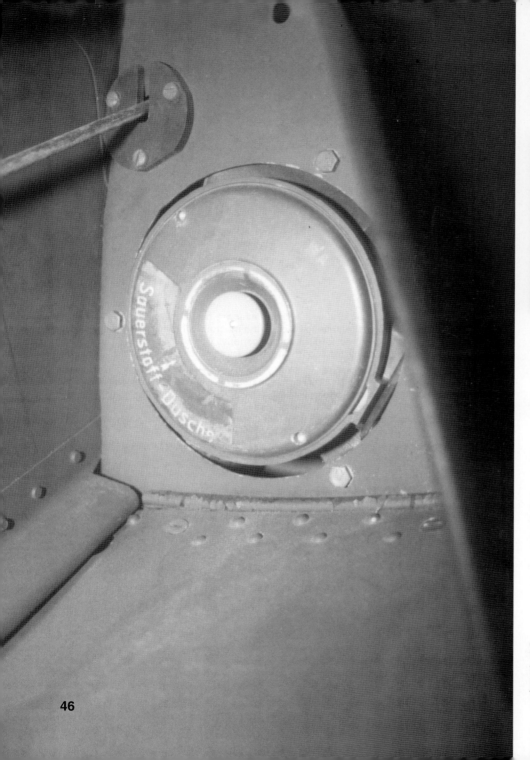

(Above) The elevator control torsion bar extends from the side of the control stick mounting base onto the starboard cockpit floor. This bar connected the stick to push rods and control cables in the fuselage, which led to the elevator differential unit and bell crank in the tail assembly. The cable on the KG 13B control stick is the electrical cord for firing the weapons via the two firing buttons on the stick. (Ryle)

Oxygen Regulator

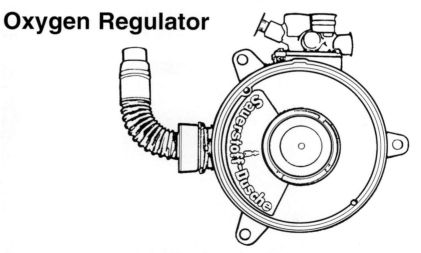

(Left) The oxygen regulator unit is mounted on the aft starboard bulkhead of the Fw 190F-8 cockpit, with the canopy jettison rod above and to the left. When the oxygen valve is opened, oxygen comes from steel bottles mounted in the aft fuselage, to the regulator unit, and into the pilot's oxygen hose. The emergency pressure button on the center of the unit could be actuated by the pilot's right elbow. (Ryle)

Hand painted in white on the starboard cockpit coaming is the warning *Achtung! Haube nur bis hier öffnen* (Attention! Open canopy only to here), referring to the red line next to this warning. The silver bar underneath the coaming actuates the firing pin for the canopy jettison system's explosive charge (Ryle)

The Fw 190F-8's forward armored windshield is set at a 25° angle and is 50MM (2 inches) thick. All three panes are set in a steel windshield frame and secured with a screwed on molded framing. The hole for the canopy spike is fitted on the upper rear of the windshield framing. (Ryle)

The Revi 16B optical reflector gun sight operated via the Fw 190F-8's 24V electrical system and has both a dimmer switch and a tinted glass plate, along with a night filter. This sight was used for both fixed weapons (cowling and wing) and bombing. The rectangular slot in the instrument panel shroud is a hand grip. (Ryle)

The piping for the Fw 190F-8's windshield deicing system was attached to the windshield by brackets secured with molded frame screws. The cooling/smoke vent for the two 13MM MG 131 machine guns is placed in the aft edge of the cowling gun cover. (Ryle)

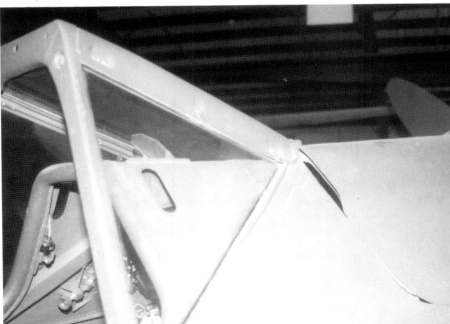

The Fw 190F-8 wing was almost identical to the A-8's, apart from the F-8's added gun breech bulges. The NASM painted their F-8 in RLM 70 (Black Green)/75 (Gray Violet) after determining this was the color scheme applied when this Fw 190A-4 was rebuilt to F-8 standard. The yellow underwing chevron arms have overlapped onto the upper port wing. The two sets of broken lines on the inboard wing surface indicate the wing walk area. Further outboard is the fabric covered aileron and its ground adjustable trim tab. (Ryle)

The wing flaps are interchangeable for either wing – this is the port wing flap – and are electrically actuated via push buttons on the port cockpit console. The three flap settings are: flight (up), take-off (13°), and landing (58°). The position of the flaps could be determined by the lights on the console, or by the mechanical reading displayed through the upper wing surface. (Ryle)

A ground adjustable trim tab is fitted on the aileron of the Fw 190F-8's port wing. The stenciling says *Nicht Verstellen* (roughly, Do not adjust). The holes at the trim tab attachment point to the wing allow the cloth covering to wrap around the rear edge of the metal framed aileron. An identical trim tab appears on the starboard aileron. (Ryle)

Each Fw 190 aileron is attached to the wing by three fittings; this is the center fitting under the port wing. These fittings allowed for some variation in size or location in attaching the aileron, due to the numerous sub contractors producing ailerons and other small parts for the Fw 190. (Ryle)

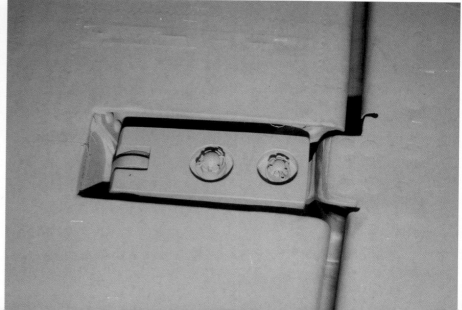

The pitot tube mounted on the Fw 190F-8's starboard wing tip measures dynamic air pressure to acquire the airspeed. The bronze tip can be electrically heated (via a switch in the cockpit) to prevent freezing and ice from closing the pitot's tip hole. Earlier Fw 190s mounted this tube just outboard of the starboard wing cannon. (Ryle)

The Fw 190F-8's starboard wingtip navigation light is green; a red light appears on the port wingtip. The F series used a rounder navigation light than the teardrop-shaped style lights employed by earlier Fw 190s. The original design was interchangeable with these later lights. The rear of the light has been painted over with RLM 75 Gray-Violet. The stenciling C3 refers to the electrical harness code for the light. (Ryle)

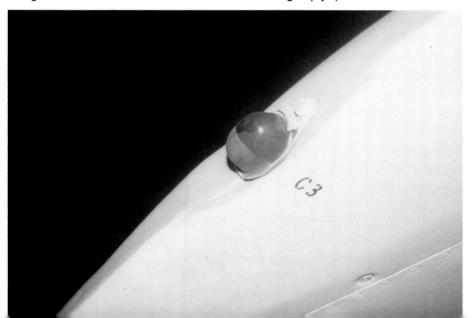

The Fw 190F-8's pitot tube is attached to the formed wingtip cover on the starboard wing's leading edge. Static air pressure required for pressure altitude is measured at the base of the pitot tube. The raised red and white landing gear indicator indicated to the pilot and ground crew the starboard main gear is locked in the extended position. (Ryle)

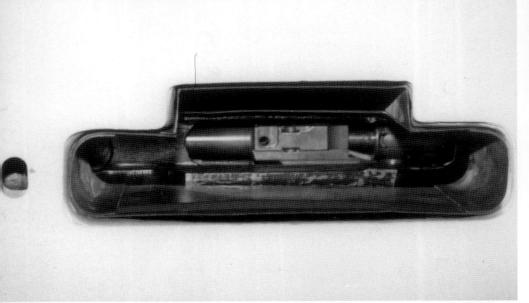

The left wing-root 20MM cannon ejection port is shaped to allow both spent cartridge casings and ammunition belt links to exit the wing bottom The small hole aft of the port facilitates access to the mounting screw inside the wing. Another such port appears under the starboard wing-root cannon. (Ryle)

The access door for the wing-root 20MM ammunition boxes was located just aft of the wheel well in the lower fuselage. This door opens from outboard and hangs down at the center while the 250-round ammunition boxes are loaded. The ETC 501 rack must be swung down to access these boxes. The stencil says, roughly: Before removing boxes detach feed (neck) collar. (Ryle)

The gun camera window is fitted into the leading edge of the Fw 190F-8's port wing. The camera was fitted into the wheel well with the lens looking through the circular window. The camera is not fitted to this aircraft. This F-8 used a 'Robot' Model II miniature camera, operated by a button on the throttle lever. The Fw 190 could also employ the BSK 16, which started and stopped by pressing the firing button on the control stick. (Ryle)

Fw 190A/F Inboard Wing Under Surface

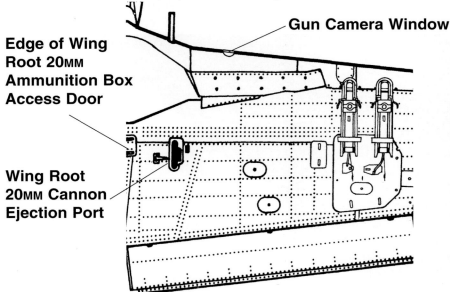

Gun Camera Window

Edge of Wing Root 20MM Ammunition Box Access Door

Wing Root 20MM Cannon Ejection Port

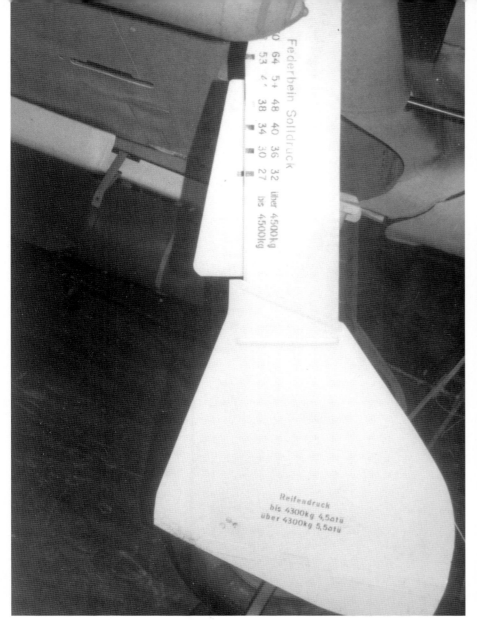

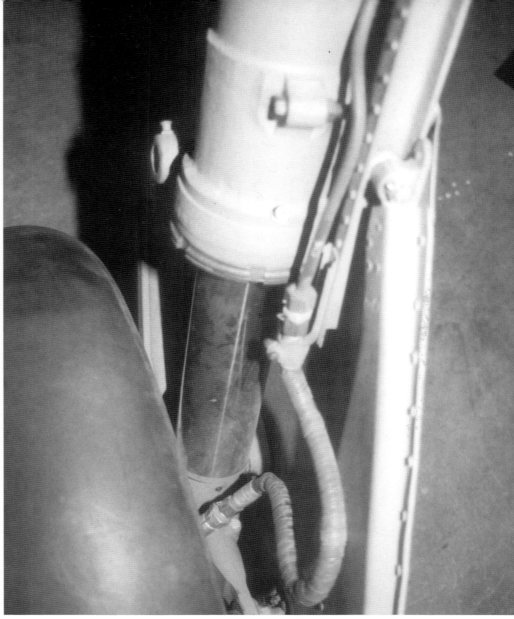

The Fw 190F-8 starboard upper landing gear door is bolted to the main gear strut. The bolt heads are placed in recessed areas of the outside door surface and covered with cloth before painting in the undersurface color. The stenciling on the upper gear door indicated gear strut pressures in atmospheres for different aircraft weights, while the lower door stenciling lists tire pressure in atmospheres for different aircraft weights. These stencils were used on Fw 190s from the A-7 onward. (Ryle)

The brake line runs down the front of the oleo strut of the Fw 190F-8's port main landing gear; a similar line appears on the starboard main gear. This brake line – in a brown anodized aluminum tube – connects to a flexible hose, which allows for strut travel, and then leads to the 300mm (11.8 inch) diameter brakes. The all-rubber tire fitted to this aircraft is of a late war design, which does not have a tread pattern. (Ryle)

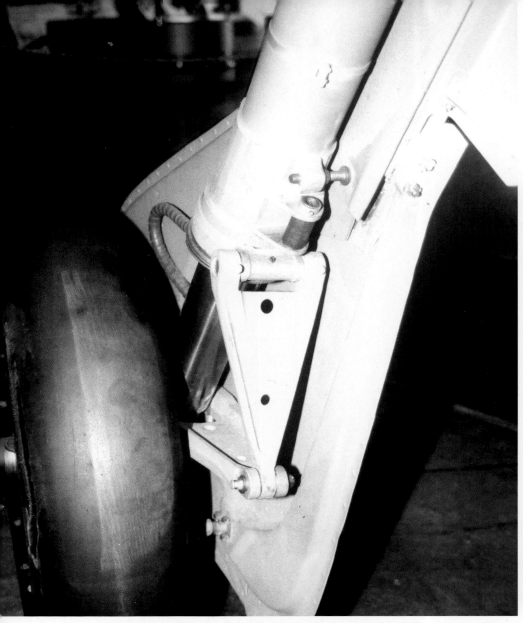

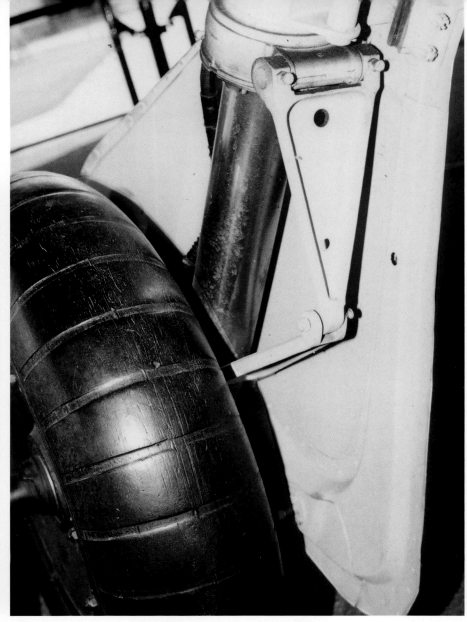

The main landing gear scissor link was attached to the rear of both the upper and lower shock strut sections. These scissors absorbed torque stresses and kept the main wheel correctly aligned. The oleo strut between the scissor arms functioned as a shock absorber to lessen the forces associated with landing and taxiing. The small round fitting immediately above the scissors is the shock strut spur used to lock the main landing gear in the up position. (Ryle)

The Fw 190A-6's starboard landing gear is the same unit later used on the F-8. This A-6 is equipped with the more common tire used on Fw 190s. The 700 мм (27.6 inch) by 175 мм (6.9 inch) main tire has a lateral tread pattern used by Fw 190 main tires from 1941 until the end of the war. Carbon black was added to the rubber to give the dark color; this ingredient was often left out of late war tires due to supply shortages. (Ryle)

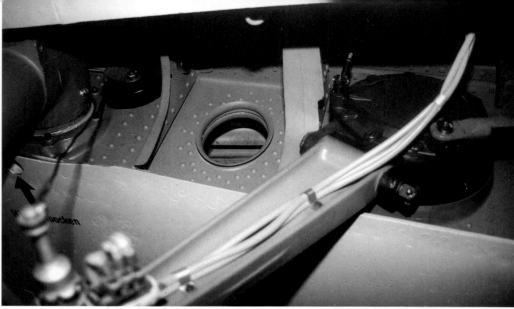

The Fw 190F-8 main wheel was forged and then machined into its final shape and size. The triangular area contains the stem for filling the tire with air. Tire pressure was based on aircraft weight at take-off: 4300 KG (9479.7 lbs), tire pressure 5.0 atmospheres (73 lbs), 4900 KG (10,802.4 lbs), tire pressure 5.5 atmospheres (81 lbs). The axle retaining nut at the hub secured the wheel to the main landing gear axle. (Ryle)

The port main landing gear upper radius strut is attached to the rotating drive on its left and the sealed air jack is attached to the drive on its right. The air jack is spring loaded and pressurized at 1400 psi. This jack worked with gravity to lower the main gear in the event of an electrical failure and then held the gear in the down position for landing. (Ryle)

The starboard main gear strut attached to the Fw 190F-8's main wing spar, which also comprised the aft main gear bay wall. The tail wheel retraction wire – attached to the upper radius strut – passes over a roller at the outboard top of the wheel well before proceeding inward along the top of the well. The upper radius strut is connected to the electrical rotating drive unit mounted in the main spar. The strut wiring is connected to the microswitch, which shuts off the drive motor when the gear is fully extended and locked. (Ryle)

The sealed air jack in the Fw 190F-8's starboard wheel well is mounted to the main wing spar at the same cross-member used for the up-lock mechanism. Electrical and brake lines for the wing run along the front of the wheel well, while the tail wheel wire runs along the aft side of the well. (Ryle)

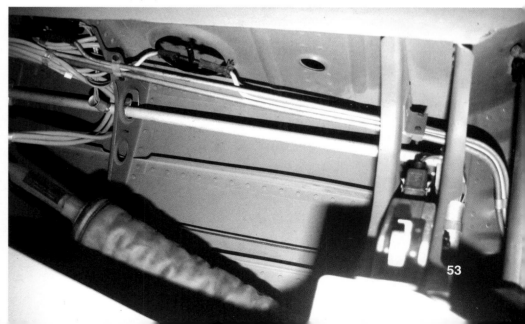

53

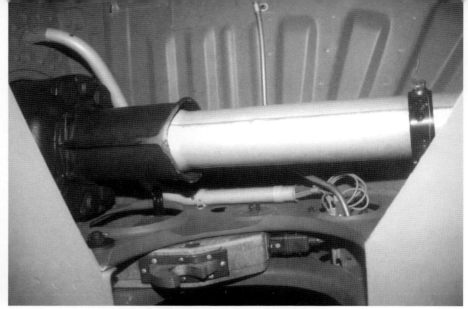

The main gear locking unit and sealed air jack are mounted on the aft wall of the starboard Fw 190F-8 wheel well. The electrical locking unit's hook grabbed the shock strut spur on the rear of the main strut to lock the main gear in the up position. This hook electrically released the spur when the gear was lowered. The unit automatically shuts off the drive motor when the hook contacts the oleo spurs and locks the gear upward. (Ryle)

The dimple pattern internal wheel cover is installed in the starboard wheel well. This panel covers the tail wheel retraction wire and some electrical wiring which exits the well. The wheel cover rear does not extend to the wheel well's aft wall. The cowling machine gun ammunition boxes would be installed in the open area at the aft edge of the cover. The wing-root 20mm cannon blast tube is outboard of the wheel cover. (Ryle)

The barrel of the port wing-root 20mm cannon is contained in a blast tube located in the wheel well. The non-adjustable forward mount is placed in the aft wall around the tube, while the barrel support clamp is fitted at the front wall. The landing gear locking unit hook is located beside the blast tube. This hook has a slight downward cant when not holding the oleo spurs. The bundled wiring passes into the main wing spar. (Ryle)

The ammunition box guide brackets for the cowl-mounted 13mm MG 131 machine guns are attached to the fuselage firewall above the main wing spar. The ammunition boxes extended into the wheel well and used a hinged belt and cartridge casing chute (not installed), which extended through the wheel well to the two cowling gun ejection ports in the wing under surface. This photograph shows the area immediately above the wheel well cover in the preceeding photograph. (Ryle)

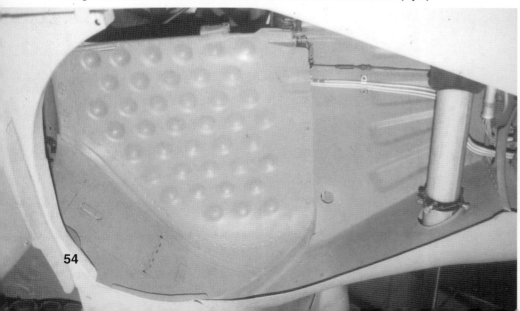

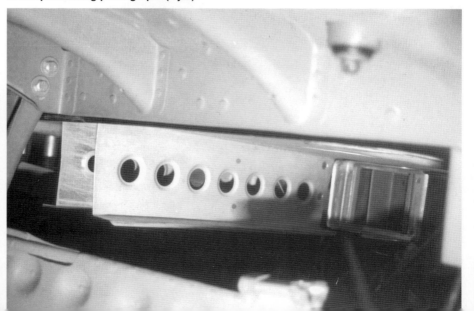

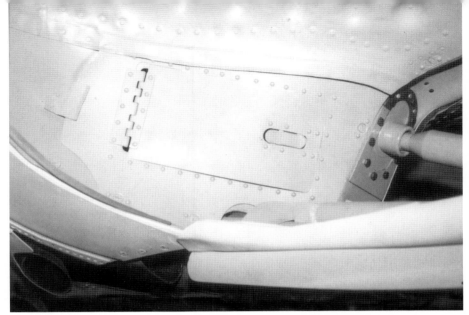

(Above) The lower engine mount and its cover are located in the center of the Fw 190F-8 wheel well. The two access doors of the unit's cover are not the same size and allow access to the lower aft section of the engine. A flush-fitting latch secures the access door to the wheel well and this door turns on a piano hinge. The wheel wells and inner surfaces of landing gear doors were painted RLM 02 Gray (FS36165) – the standard color used for the interior components of German aircraft during World War II. (Ryle)

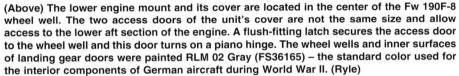

(Above Right) The aft wall of the wheel well and the fuselage firewall in the Fw 190A-6 was identical to this area of the F-8. The internal wheel covers are not installed, allowing access to the bottom of the engine accessory section. These accessories included fuel pumps and feed lines, hydraulic lines, and electrical wiring for the BMW 801D-2 engine. The wheel door upper strut is attached just outboard of the cowling gun ammunition box area. (Ryle)

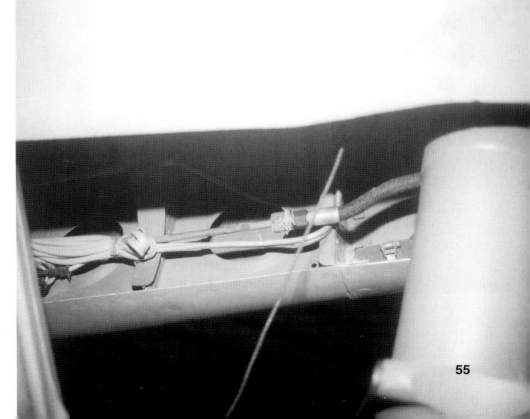

(Right) Electrical wiring and hydraulic tubing run along the forward wall of the Fw 190F-8's starboard wheel well. This includes the flexible upper hose section of the brake system, which is connected by a hose fitting to the tubing. (Ryle)

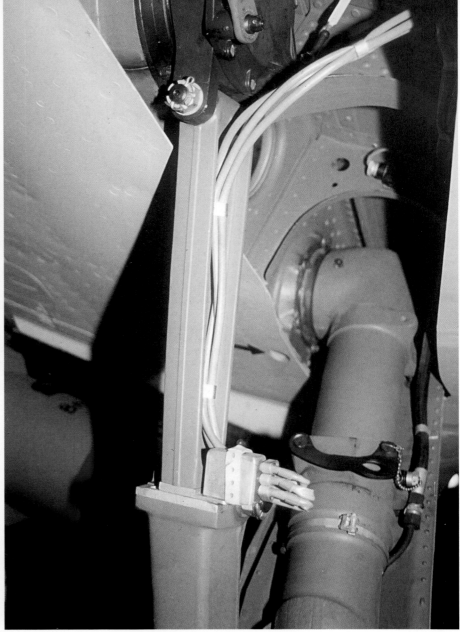

The wiring for the upper radius strut microswitch and the brake piping runs along the upper outboard section of the port wheel well. The electrical circuits have hand painted codes. The electrical plug in the well's upper center is for the gun camera (not installed). The white lower portion of the landing gear indicator rod is to the right of the rotating drive and extends through the wing at the top of the wheel well. (Ryle)

The rotating drive, upper radius strut, and main landing gear strut are mounted on the main spar. A microswitch was fitted at the bottom of the upper radius strut. When the upper and lower radius strut reached its full extension after the landing gear locked down, the microswitch turned off the drive motor. The towing attachment for ground movement of the aircraft is placed on the main gear strut. (Ryle)

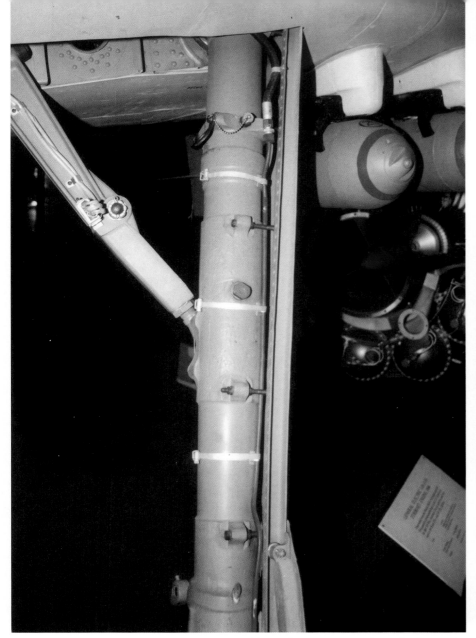

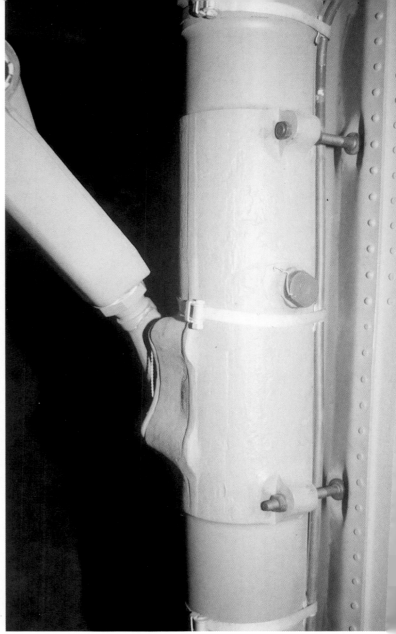

The aluminum brake line ran the front length of the main gear strut and attached to a rubber hose at the top and bottom of the strut. This allowed the brake line flexibility when the gear was raised and lowered and the shock strut flexed up and down. The radius strut intersected with the aft main gear strut. Two 110.2 pound (50 KG) SC50 bombs are mounted outboard of the port landing gear. (Ryle)

The Fw 190F-8 main landing gear strut is of a pattern used from early throu̲ duction Fw 190s. This unit is made with forged and machined steel. It does tags attached to the gear leg. The anodized aluminum brake line runs bet̲ and the gear cover and is attached to the strut with three retaining straps.

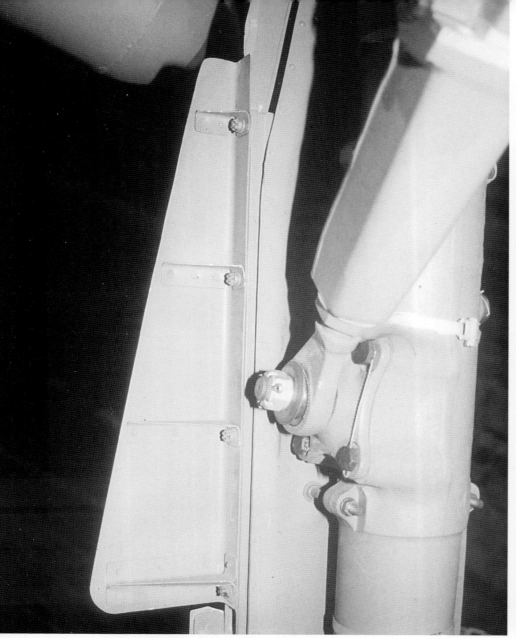

The lower radius strut was attached to a point on the aft side of the main landing gear strut. The lower and upper radius struts maintained the main gear struts' proper angle when extended. The main landing gear door was mounted to the outboard side of the main gear strut. Landing gear assemblies on German aircraft in World War II were normally painted RLM 02 Gray. (Ryle)

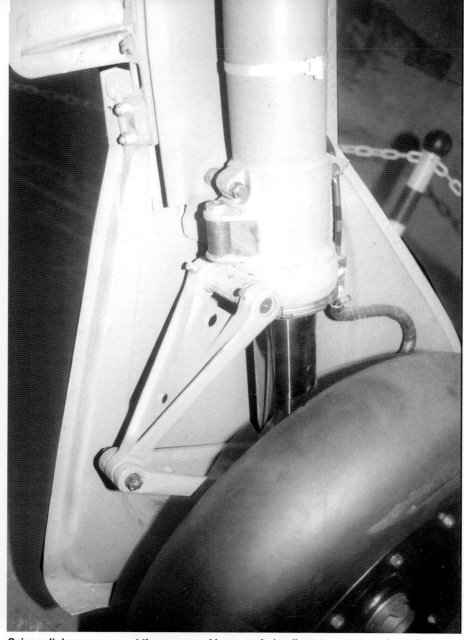

Scissor link arms connect the upper and lower main landing gear strut sections. The scissor halves are jointed to move while the oleo strut extends or compresses with the forces placed upon it. The oleo strut – compressed with aircraft weight on the ground – is chromed for ease of movement within the main gear strut. (Ryle)

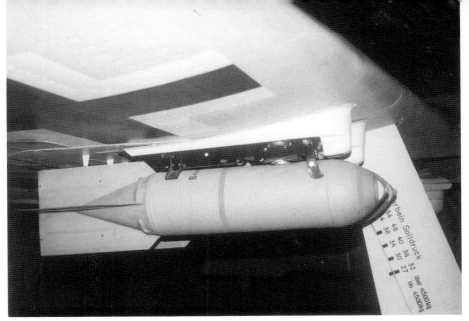

A 110.2 pound (50 KG) SC50 bomb is mounted on each of the two ETC 50 bomb racks under the Fw 190F-8's starboard wing. The two racks are located just outboard of the main gear, close to the leading edge of the wing. Two additional ETC 50 racks are located under the port wing. (Ryle)

The ETC 50 bomb carrier unit and the swap braces securing the bomb to the rack are painted RLM 66 Black Gray (FS36081). The fairing is painted the wing under surface color of RLM 76 Light Blue (FS36473). The bombs were painted brown – a non-standard German ordnance color – with red bands and black stenciling. Late in the war, German aircraft bombs were painted in any color available to ground personnel. (Ryle)

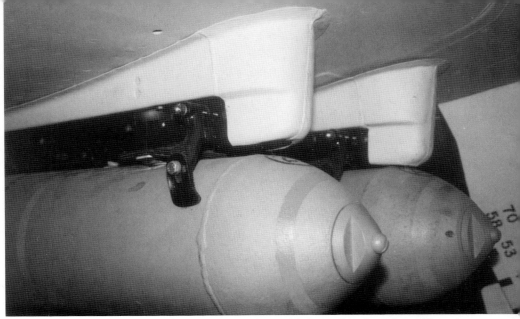

The ETC 50 fairing was a late World War II design welded together from four different stamped metal pieces. Many late-war Luftwaffe aircraft parts relied heavily on the use of welding in their manufacture, due to the low time and skill requirements of this process. The bombs are painted brown with a red stripe on the nose. (Ryle)

Electrical wiring for the ETC 50 rack ran from the carrier's aft end into the wing. The manual release lever wire extends from the wing onto the aft section of the ETC 50 rack. Installation of the Grosse Bombelektrik weapons control system allowed Fw 190F-8 pilots the option of releasing weapons selectively or in a full salvo. (Ryle)

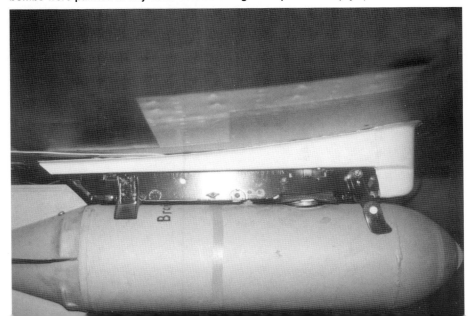

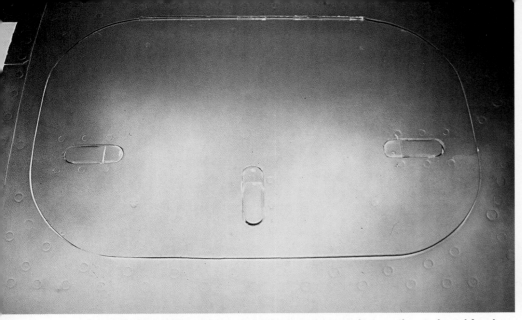

The Fw 190F-8 introduced this larger radio compartment door on the starboard fuselage side just aft of the cockpit. The door's outer shell is aluminum, and the upward-swinging panel is secured to the fuselage with three flush-fitting metal latches. Earlier Fw 190s had a smaller radio compartment door. (Ryle)

The FuG (*Funk Geräte*; Radio Device) 16Z-S radio set was introduced to the Fw 190 family with the Fw 190F-8. This radio enabled pilots to communicate with both other pilots and ground forces commanders. The FuG 16Z-S exterior is primarily painted RLM 66 Black Gray. (Ryle)

The inner shell of the radio compartment door was made of varnished wood due to the reduced availability of aluminum and other strategic materials in Germany late in World War II. The door's manufacturer affixed a small data tag decal to the aft side of the door interior. (Ryle)

The FuG 16Z-S radio is placed in front of the Fw 190F-8's aft cockpit bulkhead, with wiring conduits placed nearby. The electrical wiring went through the bulkhead to the antenna and remote compass in the aft fuselage. (Ryle)

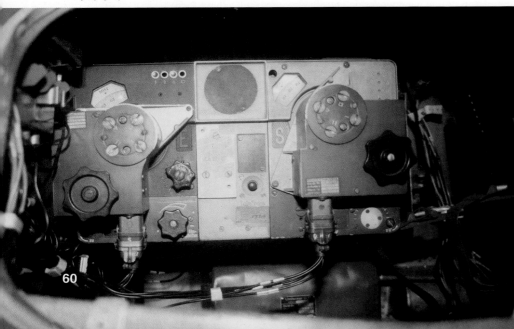

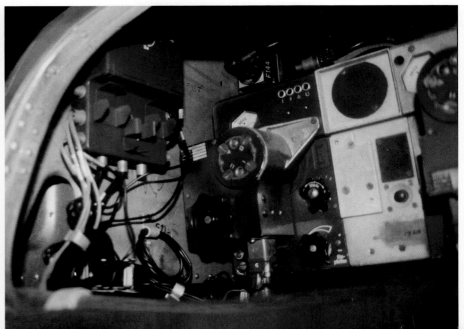

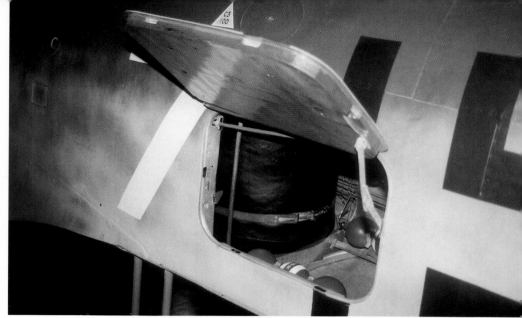

(Above) The FuG 16Z-S radio is placed immediately aft of the cockpit in the Fw 190F-8. The rear of the pilot's seat blocks off the front end of the radio compartment. Battery box hold-down straps are installed aft of the seat. The FuG 16Z-S was a VHF (Very High Frequency) radio for voice and radio homing communications and was used by ground attack pilots for both communications and target approach. (Ryle)

(Above Right) The Fw 190F-8 port fuselage access door is located aft of the cockpit. This door has an outer shell of aluminum and an inner surface of laminated wood. The black 115 liter (30.4 gallon) auxiliary fuel tank in the forward portion of this compartment was optional equipment on this aircraft. The tank is coated with a self-sealing compound, which – when punctured by projectiles or shrapnel – immediately swells to close the hole and prevent fires and explosions. The blue spherical items aft of the fuel tank are oxygen bottles. (Ryle)

(Right) The Fw 190F-8's lower fuselage access panel was built with laminated wood – a common occurrence late in World War II, due to shortages in aluminum and other strategic materials. The auxiliary fuel tank is placed forward of the panel. Oxygen bottles were mounted alongside the port and starboard sides of this lower panel. Oxygen from these bottles was fed to the pilot's oxygen mask to enable the pilot to breathe at high altitudes. The fuselage interior was anodized to fight corrosion; however, it is not painted. (Ryle)

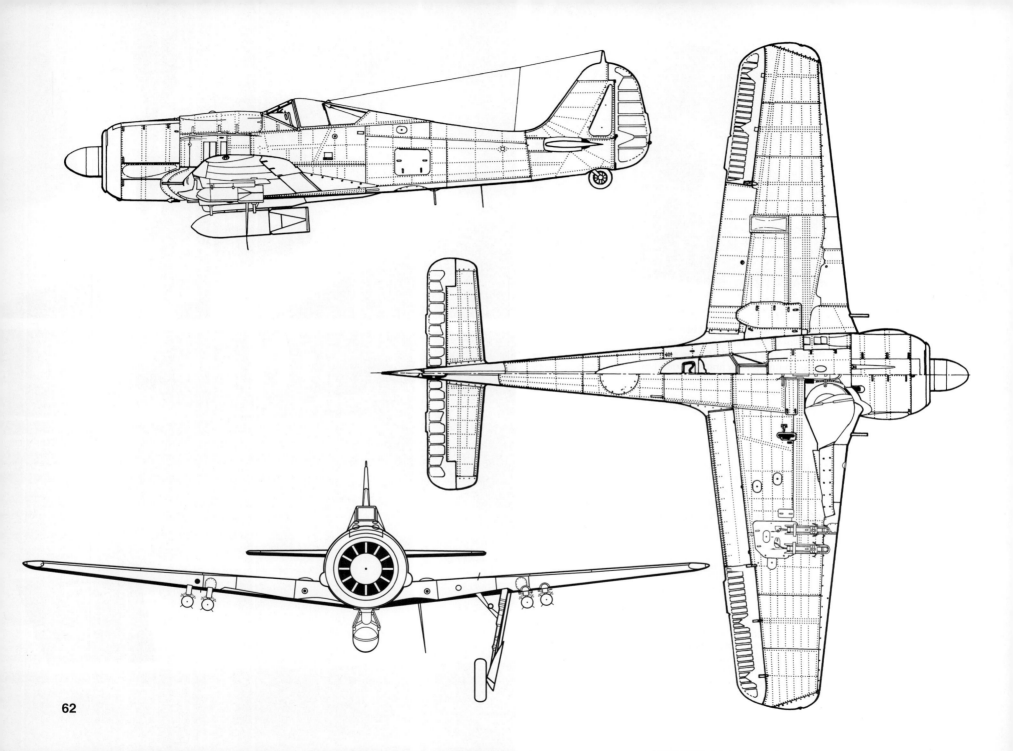

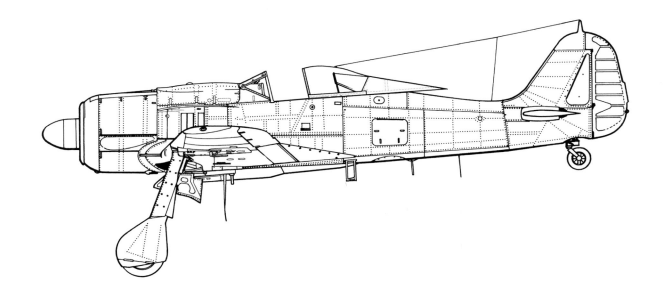

Focke-Wulf Fw 190F-8 Specifications

Wingspan: 34 feet 5 inches (10.49 м)
Length: 29 feet 4 inches (8.94 м)
Height: 12 feet 11 inches (3.94 м)
Empty Weight: 8346.56 pounds (3786 кг)
Maximum Weight: 12,067.9 pounds (5474 кг)
Powerplant: One 1730 hp BMW 801D-2 twin-row, 14 cylinder, air-cooled radial engine

Armament: Two fuselage-mounted 13мм MG 131 machine guns with 400-475 rounds per gun; two wing root 20мм MG 151/20E cannons with 250 rounds per gun; one 1102.3 lb (500 кг) or four 110.2 lb (50 кг) bombs on centerline rack; four 110.2 lb (50кг) bombs on underwing racks
Maximum Speed: 412.6 mph (664 кмн) at 21,981.6 feet (6700 м)
Service Ceiling: 33,989.5 feet (10,360 м)
Maximum Range: 851.3 miles (1370 км)

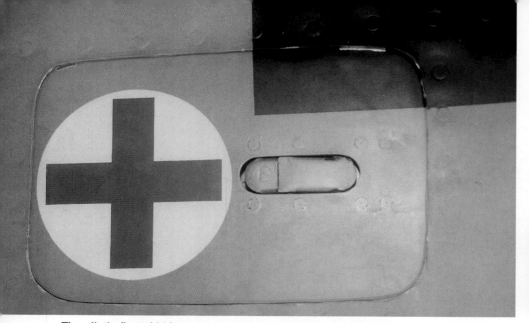

The pilot's first aid kit access panel is installed on the aft starboard fuselage of the Fw 190F-8 and is identical to such panels on other Fw 190 variants, although the location moved on the A-7 and later models. Once the flush-fitting latch is opened, this panel can be completely removed from the fuselage to obtain access to the first aid kit. (Ryle)

The opened external power connection hatch reveals the socket for the three-pronged external power plug. When the Fw 190F-8 was on the ground, 24V of external power was provided for charging the aircraft's battery – which provided electrical power in flight – and powering internal electrical systems for ground maintenance. (Ryle)

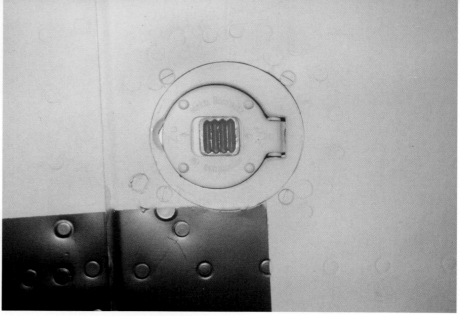

The 24-volt external power connection on the starboard aft fuselage is covered with a small flush-fitting hatch. The opening mechanism is painted red, although the entire hatch may be painted this color on some Fw 190s. The outside of the black German *Balkankreuz* (Balkan Cross) insignia is just below the power connection hatch. (Ryle)

The Fw 190F-8's rear jacking point is located on the aft fuselage just ahead of the tail section. A circular cover plate on each side covers the lift tube placed inside the fuselage. The stencil *Hier aufbocken* (Lift Below) is partially covered by the RLM 04 Yellow identification band, which also covered the black arrow pointing to the cover plate. (Ryle)

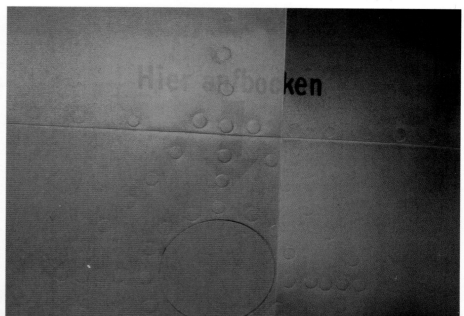

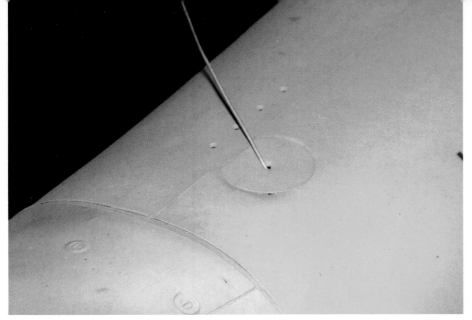

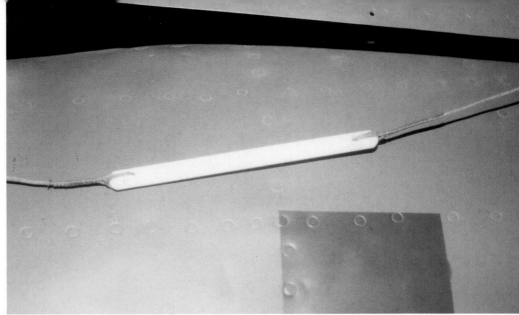

The Fw 190's vertical antenna wire entered the fuselage spine immediately ahead of the vertical stabilizer. The vertical antenna installation on this Fw 190A-6 was introduced on the A-4 variant and used on most radial-engined Fw 190s. The fuselage lead-in is offset to starboard. (Ryle)

One of the two ceramic insulators on the Fw 190F-8's main antenna wire rests against the fuselage near the open canopy. This insulator prevented radio interference from the grounding of the antenna wire to the aircraft. The antenna wire on Fw 190s fitted with 'blown' canopies falls to the aircraft's spine when the canopy is open. (Ryle)

The vertical antenna wire wraps around the main wire where they intersect directly over the fuselage spine. The main radio antenna wire extends from the top of the vertical stabilizer to the Plexiglas canopy. This metal wire allowed radio messages to be sent to and received from great distances. (Ryle)

The main antenna wire connects with the Fw 190F-8's vertical stabilizer through a tensioning spring. This spring maintained proper wire tension on aircraft equipped with both 'flat' and 'blown' canopies. The vertical antenna mast introduced on the Fw 190A-4 replaced the shorter fairing used on earlier Fw 190s. (Ryle)

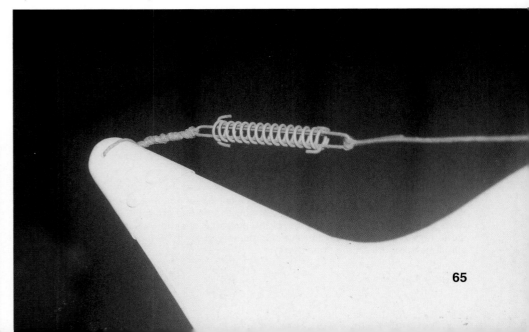

The Fw 190F-8 employed a welded steel fork tail wheel housing around the tire. The fork is bowed slightly inward. The tail wheel hub extensions are for a forked tail wheel bar, used by ground personnel to control the aircraft's direction when towed. These extensions rest in a cradle used to raise this preserved Fw 190F-8 slightly off the ground to eliminate pressure on the tires. (Ryle)

The Fw 190F-8 tail wheel has a centering lock, used to lock the wheel straight ahead on takeoff. The centering lock's actuation rod is the lower arm on the strut assembly. This lock is connected to the elevator controls and the pilot center locked the tail wheel by pulling the control stick fully aft prior to takeoff. The tail wheel will swivel a full 360° when unlocked. The spoked wheel is of the same type used on the Messerschmitt Bf 109, while the tire has a directional tread. (Ryle)

(Above) The upper arms on the Fw 190F-8 tail wheel strut assembly are drag yokes for guiding the retraction/extension of the tail wheel and acting as a stabilizer. The tail wheel was extended and retracted using a cable attached to the starboard main landing gear. The tail wheel assembly was not locked in the up position, but held in place by the cable. When extended, a lock-down fitting was wedged into a cavity at the base of the shock strut guide and held there by the attached spring, which kept the tail wheel extended. (Ryle)

(Right) The Fw 190F-8 tail assembly was virtually unchanged on radial engined Fw 190s throughout the war. The tall antenna mast replaced the shorter antenna housing on the Fw 190A-4. The rudder was attached to the vertical stabilizer by three pivot bearings, although held in place by small bolts at the center point/actuation lever. The light colored section of the main antenna wire is a ceramic insulator. Only the last three numbers of the W.Nr. (*Werk Nummer*; Factory Number) were painted in black on the starboard side of the stabilizer – a common practice in the Luftwaffe. (Mautner)

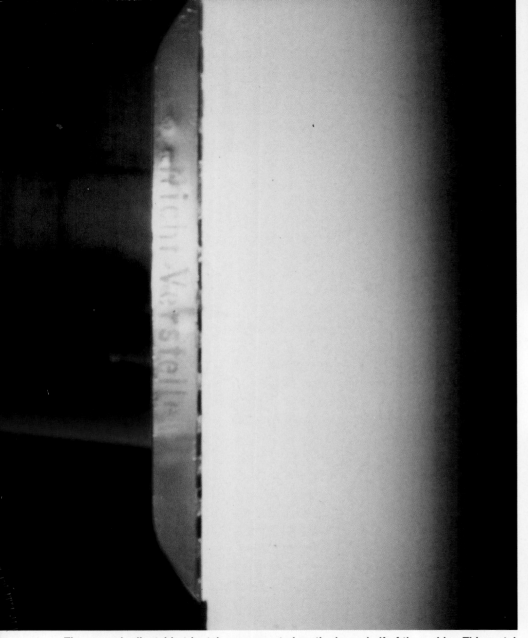

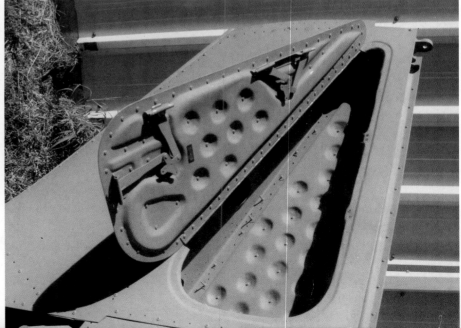

The full *Werk Nummer* (Factory Number) of this Fw 190F-8 is painted on the port vertical stabilizer. The position of the hand-painted number – at the top of the stabilizer – was the most common location of this item on Fw 190s. The top of the tail wheel strut access door is located just below the upper portion of the rudder. (Ryle)

The tail wheel strut access door is open on an Fw 190 vertical stabilizer under restoration at Rio Hondo, Texas. The waffle pattern stiffening panels on the tail inner surfaces were common to all Fw 190s. Two door locking mechanisms were installed to secure the door closed for flight. A decal data tag was applied above the lower lock. (Houston)

The ground adjustable trim tab was mounted on the lower half of the rudder. This metal trim tab was identical in size, shape, and attachment to other such trim tabs on most Fw 190s. The white stenciling on the red tab reads: *Nicht Verstellen* (Do Not Adjust). Trim tabs on an aircraft's control surfaces hold the main surface – rudder, elevator, or aileron – in the desired neutral position for flight under various air loads. (Ryle)

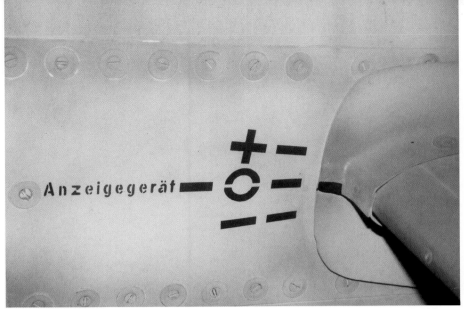

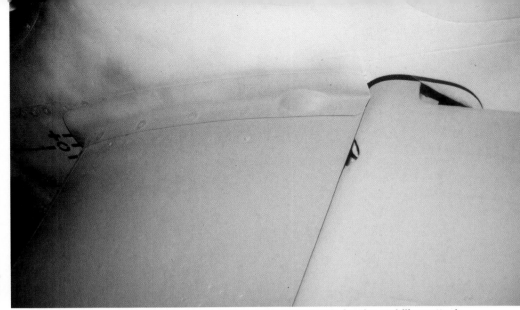

The stenciling at the leading edge of the port horizontal stabilizer indicates the incidence limits, with *Anzeigegerät* (Gauge) printed along the centerline. The Fw 190's pilot could electrically adjust the stabilizer incidence a total of 5° to compensate for changes in the aircraft's fore-and-aft trim (balance in flight). The electrical trim motor was located in the base of the vertical stabilizer. (Ryle)

A blister atop the horizontal stabilizer fairing allowed clearance for the stabilizer attachment fitting. The horizontal stabilizer attachment point secured this section to the Fw 190's airframe, yet allowed movement to adjust its incidence. The elevator's travel range was +30° to -25° from neutral. (Ryle)

Fw190S-8, W.Nr. 584219, Black 38, is on display at the Royal Air Force Museum in Hendon, England. The aircraft is marked with JG 54 insignia. R. Sochor *Fabrik* in Blanz-Blansko, Poland converted an Fw 190F-8/U1 single-seat fighter into a two-seat trainer (S-8) in late 1944. After being surrendered at Grove, Germany in the spring of 1945, it was ferried to Farnborough, England on 2 September 1945. In May of 1946 the Fw 190S-8 was consid-

ered unusual enough to be selected by the Air Ministry Air Historical Branch for preservation. The aircraft was moved several times and received the Air Ministry 29 (AM29) designation along the way. Transferred to RAF St. Athan, England in 1974, the aircraft was allocated RAF Ground Instructional serial No. 8470M. The engine was run several times during the aircraft's stay at St. Athan. (Ranger)

The Fw 190S-8 forward cockpit is much like a standard late war Fw 190 cockpit; however, a few items are different. The two-seater lacks a gun sight, advanced navigation equipment, weapon round counters, and the oxygen system. The handful of two-seat Fw 190Ss produced served as conversion trainers with ground attack units operating the Fw 190F and G and in Luftwaffe advanced flight schools. (Ranger)

Fw 190S-5

Fw 190S-8

The forward (student) cockpit canopy of the Fw 190S-8 opened upwards and hinged to starboard. The right canopy section remained fixed to the airframe. The cable connecting the moving and fixed portions of the canopy kept the canopy from flopping completely over. The Fw 190S-5 and S-8 were two-seat conversions of the Fw 190A-5 and A-8/F-8, respectively. (Ranger)

The instructor occupied the aft cockpit of the Fw 190S-8. The aft cockpit was built into the fuselage by extending the canopy into two sections and extending the cockpit aft to install the second crew station. The canvas seat belts are white, with the shoulder straps attached to a steel bar immediately aft of the seat back. A brown leather seat cushion is installed, while the control stick has a wooden grip. (Ranger)

The throttle of the Fw 190F-8/U-1 (S-8) was similar in size and placement on the port console to the forward cockpit. The white T-shaped handle forward of and above the throttle is the landing gear release lever, which allowed the instructor to extend the gear for landing. The side consoles were painted RLM 66 Black Gray. (Ranger)

The Fw 190S-8 aft cockpit was a cramped arrangement and had only the most rudimentary pilot necessities: control stick (with wooden grip), throttle, basic flight and engine instruments, starter, landing gear control, and flap control. Tubes running from the base of the control stick links with the forward cockpit and the ailerons and elevators. The instrument panel was painted RLM 66 Black Gray. (Ranger)

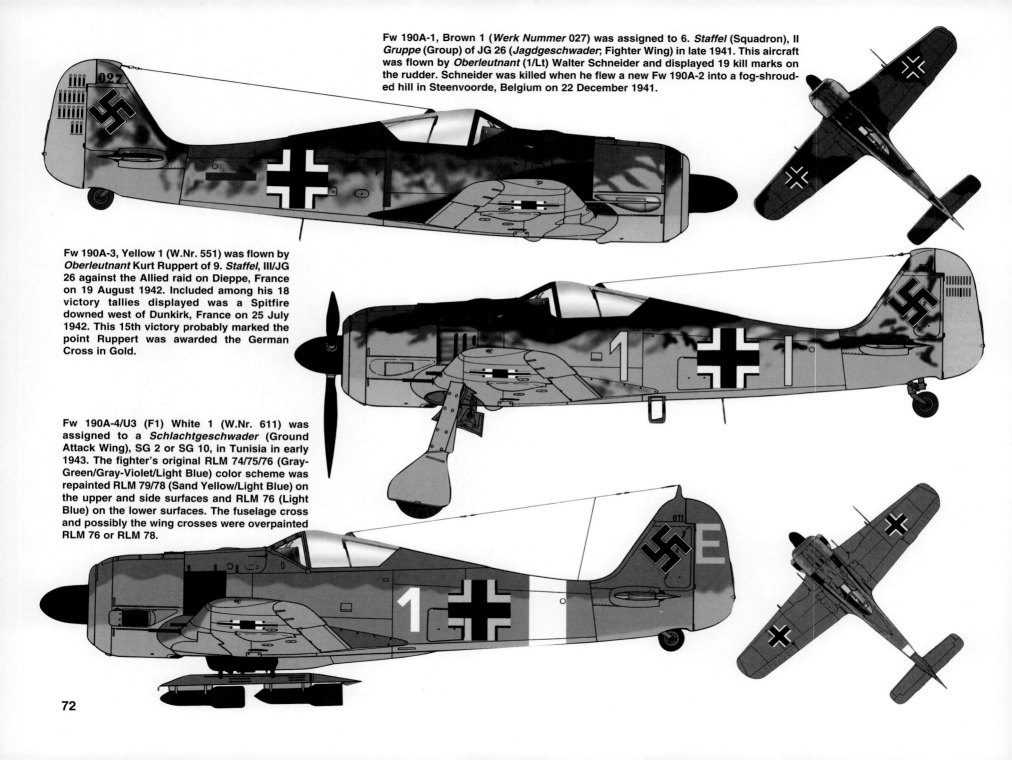

Fw 190A-1, Brown 1 (*Werk Nummer* 027) was assigned to 6. *Staffel* (Squadron), II *Gruppe* (Group) of JG 26 (*Jagdgeschwader*; Fighter Wing) in late 1941. This aircraft was flown by *Oberleutnant* (1/Lt) Walter Schneider and displayed 19 kill marks on the rudder. Schneider was killed when he flew a new Fw 190A-2 into a fog-shrouded hill in Steenvoorde, Belgium on 22 December 1941.

Fw 190A-3, Yellow 1 (W.Nr. 551) was flown by *Oberleutnant* Kurt Ruppert of 9. *Staffel*, III/JG 26 against the Allied raid on Dieppe, France on 19 August 1942. Included among his 18 victory tallies displayed was a Spitfire downed west of Dunkirk, France on 25 July 1942. This 15th victory probably marked the point Ruppert was awarded the German Cross in Gold.

Fw 190A-4/U3 (F1) White 1 (W.Nr. 611) was assigned to a *Schlachtgeschwader* (Ground Attack Wing), SG 2 or SG 10, in Tunisia in early 1943. The fighter's original RLM 74/75/76 (Gray-Green/Gray-Violet/Light Blue) color scheme was repainted RLM 79/78 (Sand Yellow/Light Blue) on the upper and side surfaces and RLM 76 (Light Blue) on the lower surfaces. The fuselage cross and possibly the wing crosses were overpainted RLM 76 or RLM 78.

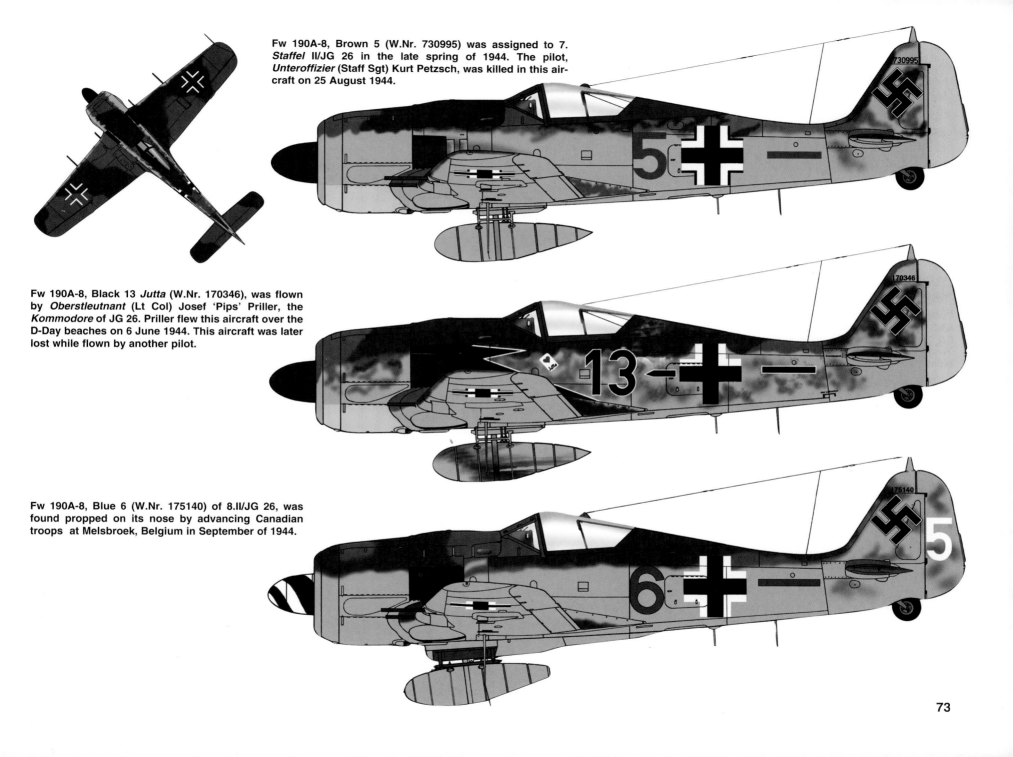

Fw 190A-8, Brown 5 (W.Nr. 730995) was assigned to 7. *Staffel* II/JG 26 in the late spring of 1944. The pilot, *Unteroffizier* (Staff Sgt) Kurt Petzsch, was killed in this aircraft on 25 August 1944.

Fw 190A-8, Black 13 *Jutta* (W.Nr. 170346), was flown by *Oberstleutnant* (Lt Col) Josef 'Pips' Priller, the *Kommodore* of JG 26. Priller flew this aircraft over the D-Day beaches on 6 June 1944. This aircraft was later lost while flown by another pilot.

Fw 190A-8, Blue 6 (W.Nr. 175140) of 8.II/JG 26, was found propped on its nose by advancing Canadian troops at Melsbroek, Belgium in September of 1944.

Personnel of the 93rd Fighter Squadron, 81st Fighter Group captured this rare Fw190A-4/U3, White 1/Yellow E (W.Nr. 611) in Tunisia in 1943. This aircraft was assigned to either SG 2 or SG 10 and was fitted with sand filters to its engine intakes. The RLM 79 Sand Yellow upper surfaces wrap around the wing leading edges. Remains of the Fw 190's bomb rack are placed under the fuselage (Fochuk)

An Fw 190, believed to be a late-war A-8, was captured by 401 Squadron, Royal Canadian Air Force (RCAF). The aircraft's Luftwaffe markings were painted out and RCAF markings – including the letters YO for 401 Squadron – applied. The practice of Allied pilots flying captured German aircraft was forbidden after the war; propellers and rudders were removed from these aircraft to prevent unauthorized flights. (Bracken via Fochuk)

Several Fw 190s are parked on the flight line of 12. *Staffel*, IV *Gruppe*, JG 5 at Herdla, Norway in March of 1945. Fuselage codes were blue – the color assigned to 12. *Staffel* – and most of the aircraft display signs of repainting. One Fw 190 is parked in the hangar beyond the flight line. (Crow)

US troops found Fw 190A-8, Black 9 (W.Nr. 737938) on the edge of a field in Germany, once used for an air base, in 1945. The aircraft's 'blown hood' canopy and main fuel cell were removed and placed on the ground beside the Fw 190. The color variations of aircraft components – particularly on the tail assembly – resulted from the many small factories producing Fw 190 subassemblies. (Crow)

Fw 190F-8/R1, White 48 (W.Nr. 587108) was assigned to an unknown fighter unit when it was captured by US troops. The captured aircraft was parked at Lippstadt, Germany in May and June of 1945. The Fw 190's tail wheel was not fully extended or the tail wheel strut had lost pressure; however, the rest of this aircraft is in good condition. (Crow)

Fw 190A-8 (W.Nr. 171189) was assigned to (Stab) II./SG 2 when it crash landed at Kitzingen, Germany on 8 May 1945. The aircraft had a field applied camouflage scheme over the factory camouflage scheme – a frequent occurrence by the end of the war. The field-applied scheme was intended to help hide the aircraft while on the ground. Fuselage codes were black for this Fw 190A-8, which was assigned to *Major* Karl Kennel, II. *Gruppe Kommandeur*. (Crow)

Fw 190F-8, Black Chevron 4, was assigned to (*Stab*; Staff) 1./JG 301 in Germany during the spring of 1945. US troops found the aircraft in its forest airfield revetment. The Fw 190F-8's seat lay outboard of the starboard wingtip. The canopy, radio compartment access panel, and wingtip cap were removed. (Crow)

An RCAF officer perches on the cockpit sill of a captured Fw 190. This aircraft was equipped for night operations, which included the installation of flame dampers on each cylinder exhaust port. These dampers covered exhaust flames, preventing the aircraft's position from being given away and protecting the pilot's night vision. (Fochuk)

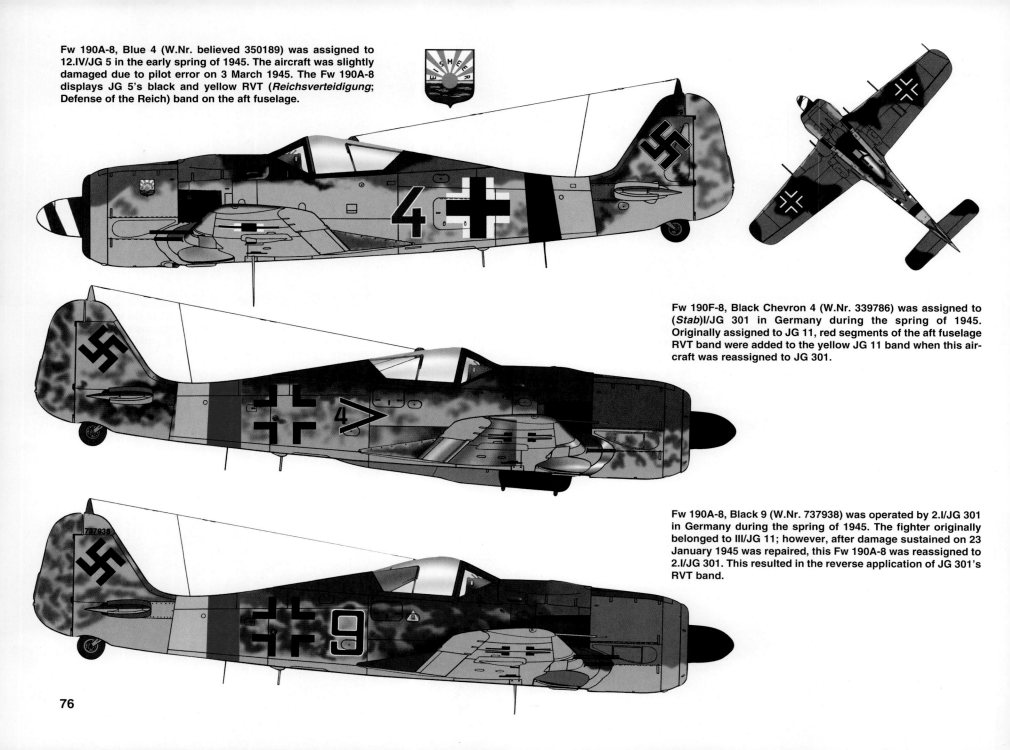

Fw 190A-8, Blue 4 (W.Nr. believed 350189) was assigned to 12.IV/JG 5 in the early spring of 1945. The aircraft was slightly damaged due to pilot error on 3 March 1945. The Fw 190A-8 displays JG 5's black and yellow RVT (*Reichsverteidigung*; Defense of the Reich) band on the aft fuselage.

Fw 190F-8, Black Chevron 4 (W.Nr. 339786) was assigned to (*Stab*)I/JG 301 in Germany during the spring of 1945. Originally assigned to JG 11, red segments of the aft fuselage RVT band were added to the yellow JG 11 band when this aircraft was reassigned to JG 301.

Fw 190A-8, Black 9 (W.Nr. 737938) was operated by 2.I/JG 301 in Germany during the spring of 1945. The fighter originally belonged to III/JG 11; however, after damage sustained on 23 January 1945 was repaired, this Fw 190A-8 was reassigned to 2.I/JG 301. This resulted in the reverse application of JG 301's RVT band.

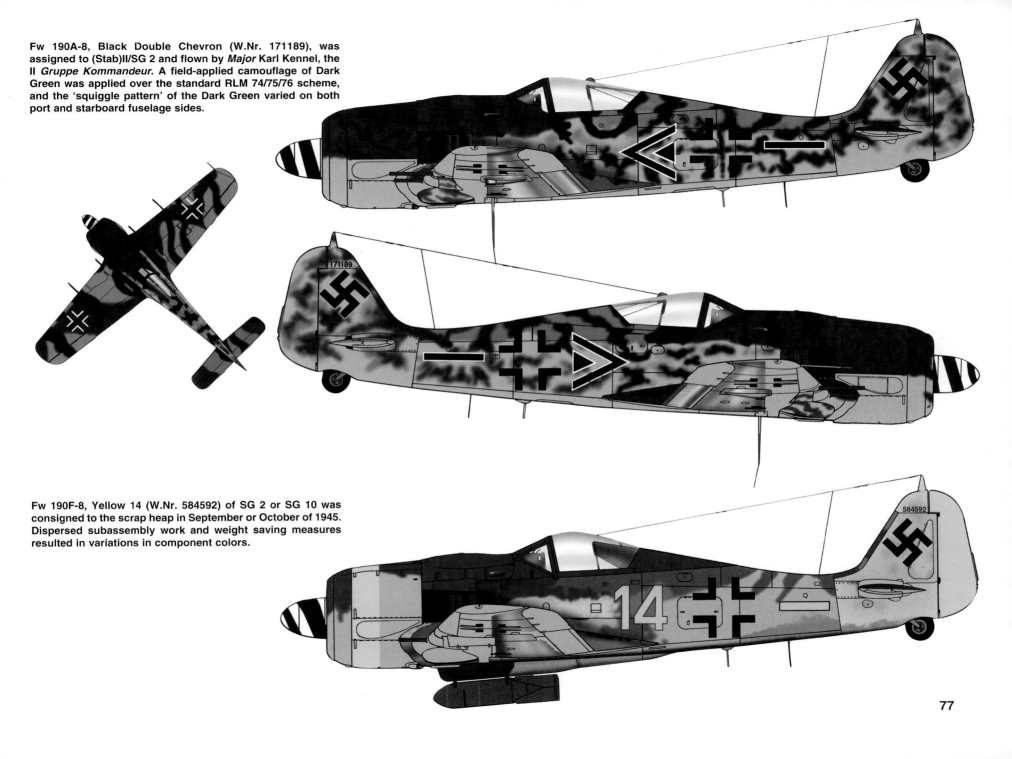

Fw 190A-8, Black Double Chevron (W.Nr. 171189), was assigned to (Stab)II/SG 2 and flown by *Major* Karl Kennel, the II *Gruppe Kommandeur*. A field-applied camouflage of Dark Green was applied over the standard RLM 74/75/76 scheme, and the 'squiggle pattern' of the Dark Green varied on both port and starboard fuselage sides.

Fw 190F-8, Yellow 14 (W.Nr. 584592) of SG 2 or SG 10 was consigned to the scrap heap in September or October of 1945. Dispersed subassembly work and weight saving measures resulted in variations in component colors.

The flaps were lowered on the same Fw 190F-8 which appeared in the previous photograph. This aircraft was assigned to either SG (*Schlachtgeschwader*; Attack Wing) 2 or SG 10 during the last months of World War II. Only half of the lower wing surfaces were painted RLM 76 Light Blue; the remainder was left in natural metal in order to save material and speed up production. (Crow)

A US MP (Military Policeman) in white helmet and three American troops stand beside Fw 190F-8/R1, White 48 (W.Nr. 587108) at Lippstadt, Germany during the spring of 1945. This is the same aircraft depicted on page 75; however, the Fw 190 was moved off the hardstand onto the field. Wing and tail national insignia are white outlined. The low tail sit on this aircraft resulted from the tail wheel strut being only partially extended or from a low presure tail wheel strut. (Crow)

Fw 190F-8, Yellow 14, (W.Nr. 584592) stands on its nose in the scrap pile at Neubiberg, Germany in the fall of 1945. This late-war production aircraft was missing its canopy and rudder, while the fuselage access panel was partially removed. Aircraft subassemblies were painted with several shades of paint, due to the dispersed manufacture of these components. (Crow)

A US solider leans on the propeller blade of an Fw 190A in Germany during the spring of 1945. A number (339786) has been painted on the lower engine cowl lip. The outboard 20MM cannons were removed from this Fw 190A to reduce weight. (Crow)

This Fw 190A-8 (W.Nr. 171189) was assigned to (*Stab*) II/SG 2 when *Major* Karl Kennel crash-landed it at Kitzingen, Germany on 8 May 1945 – the day World War II ended in Europe. Although equipped with an outboard 20MM MG151 cannon, the bulged access panel beneath the wing is associated with 30MM weapons. A second ejection chute has been cut into the 30MM panel to allow ejection of the spent 20MM shells. This is another view of the same aircraft seen on page 75. (Crow)

Two Canadian troops pose beside a nosed-over Fw 190A-8, Blue 6 (W.Nr. 175140), which was assigned to 8.II/JG 26. The under surface color of RLM 76 Light Gray wrapped around the wing's leading edge in a waved pattern. A 550 KG (1212.5 lb) bomb hidden under the Fw 190A's nose – a booby trap – exploded when the wreck was later moved by a US bull-dozer, killing several soldiers. (Harrison)

An unknown Fw 190S-8 trainer is parked on a snow-covered airfield during the winter of 1944-1945. The aircraft's spinner is painted in the RLM 21 White/22 Black spiral required for fighters from late summer of 1944 until war's end. At the same time, this Fw 190S-8 retains the early black/white crosses instead of the late 1944 style outline crosses. (Hillen via Wadman)

Butcher Birds!

More Fw 190 Titles

1170 Fw 190 in Action

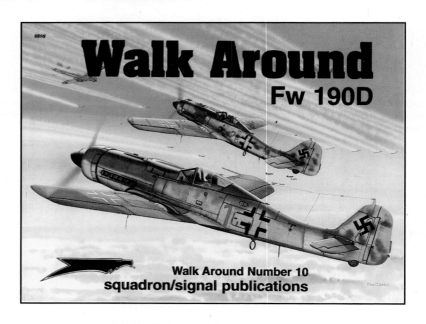

5510 Fw 190D Walk Around

from squadron/signal publications